Praise for *Welcome Homeless*

Once in a while you cross paths with someone who will forever change your life. For us, Alan Graham is that someone. His life, his heart, and his mission to see "I am" in the "least of these" is nothing less than transformative. *Welcome Homeless* is a much-needed work that gives incredible insight into how the gospel turns pain and isolation into victory and community. It's a coming home story for all of us, where we are challenged to see others as well as ourselves only as Christ sees.

—Jen and Brandon Hatmaker
Authors and Founders of The Legacy Collective

I know what homelessness feels like. I started Paul Mitchell with a $700 loan when I was living out of my car. When I met Alan Graham, I knew this was a man who really understood the problem: people need a place to belong. The Community First! Village and this book invite people into something greater, and I'm proud to be a part of it.

—John Paul DeJoria
Cofounder of Paul Mitchell and
The Patrón Spirits Company

This is a book of deep homefulness. Alan Graham is such a wonderful homemaker, in large part because he is such an evocative storyteller. Home is always a storied place and Alan tells his stories with love, gentleness, and deep, deep respect. You don't get to tell the kind of stories that we meet in this book without first going into the pain, betrayal, violence, and despair of homelessness. In this book we meet Alan's friends and mentors, and they are a stunningly beautiful cast of characters.

—Brian Walsh and Steven Bouma-Prediger
Coauthors of *Beyond Homelessness: Christian Faith in a Culture of Displacement*

Welcome Homeless is jam-packed with unabashed honesty, unfiltered stories, and profound ideas that lead you to a place of beautiful awareness about the world and the way it truly is.

—MIKE FOSTER
AUTHOR AND FOUNDER OF PEOPLE
OF THE SECOND CHANCE

Let me tell you about my friend Alan Graham. He's the man who hires a homeless friend to work at the Mobile Loaves & Fishes office, calls the police when that man steals something, and tells the man he'll be the one to pick him up when he's through serving his time in the Travis County Jail. Alan personifies Christ's command for us to be innocent as doves and shrewd as serpents. We owe him a debt we'll never repay for writing *Welome Homeless* and once again showing us all the way home.

—MAC RICHARD
LEAD PASTOR AT LAKE HILLS CHURCH

Welcome Homeless takes us on a journey seen through the eyes and heart of Alan Graham. A journey that transformed his life and, more importantly, helped transform thousands of lives over the last few decades. A journey that lets us in on the people he has met along the way—who have changed his life as much as he has now changed theirs. He has shined a light on the invisible, the unwanted, the misunderstood, and the forgotten in the most heartwarming way—through their own life stories of loss of home, family and friends, self-respect and dignity. Yet, they seem closer to God than many of us who have all those things. This book is about Love. It's about community. It's about giving. It's about relationships—first with God and then with all His children.

—JUDY TRABULSI
COFOUNDER OF GSD&M

The ministry Alan Graham has launched is nothing short of life-changing. His chronicle of the stories of the people he serves helps all of us see the homeless with new eyes and as God Himself sees them.

—KAREN HUGHES
AUTHOR AND FORMER COUNSELOR TO
PRESIDENT GEORGE W. BUSH

Welcome Homeless is a book that rattles you to your spiritual senses and awakens the awe you've been missing in your relationship with God by inviting you to love your neighbor as yourself.

—SUSIE DAVIS
AUTHOR OF *UNAFRAID*

This is one man's journey of discovering how most stories that have gone offtrack are a result of hopelessness. As a pastor in Austin, Texas, I am proud to witness firsthand the impact that Mobile Loaves & Fishes and Community First! Village is having on our city. My prayer is that this book will ignite your heart to be a part of something that only God can pull off where you live!

—BRAD THOMAS
LEAD PASTOR AT AUSTIN RIDGE BIBLE CHURCH

Welcome Homeless is a gift that takes down the walls of isolation and shows us the power of empathy and action. The real-life stories that Alan Graham shares over the course of his journey could stop a speeding train. It stopped me. The most compelling lesson Graham retaught me is that when we breathe new purpose into our own journey—when we stop, listen, connect, and share, even just for a moment—that mighty pause for humanity is one of God's most generous endowments. Thank you Alan Graham for your life's work.

—ROY SPENCE
COFOUNDER & CHAIRMAN, GSD&M
COFOUNDER & CEO, THE PURPOSE INSTITUTE

In this groundbreaking work, Alan Graham shatters our perceptions of the homeless—why they are homeless, and what society's solution to homelessness should be. Graham challenges us to see the ultimate cause of homelessness beyond what we traditionally have accepted: job loss, addiction, mental illness. Instead, Graham shows us homelessness is the irrevocable rending in the fabric of family and community that allows the homeless to fall. Graham teaches us not to simply address symptoms of homelessness, but to respond as Christ would: to welcome them home as valued members of our community and beloved brothers and sisters.

—Will Davis
Senior Pastor at Austin Christian Fellowship

WELCOME HOME~~LESS~~

WELCOME
HOMELESS

ONE MAN'S JOURNEY OF DISCOVERING
THE MEANING OF HOME

ALAN GRAHAM

WITH LAUREN HALL

W PUBLISHING GROUP

AN IMPRINT OF THOMAS NELSON

Published in Nashville, Tennessee, by W Publishing, an imprint of Thomas Nelson.

Published in association with the literary agency of The FEDD Agency, Inc., Post Office Box 341973, Austin, Texas 78734.

Thomas Nelson titles may be purchased in bulk for educational, business, fund-raising, or sales promotional use. For information, please e-mail SpecialMarkets@ ThomasNelson.com.

Library of Congress Control Number: 2016917858

ISBN 978-0-7180-8655-8

Printed in the United States of America

HB 07.26.2019

For Tricia and Mom

The LORD God then took the man and settled him in the garden of Eden, to cultivate and care for it.

—GENESIS 2:15 NAB

CONTENTS

INTRODUCTION

The Gospel Con Carne

HERE WE ARE IN THE MIDDLE OF NOWHERE, WITH SANDY cracked ground and hilly mountaintops, in the center of Hidalgo. It's that quiet moment right before the sun rises on the red hills of Mexico. An impoverished Juan Diego eagerly awakes to make his way to Mass, feeling all fifty-seven years in his bones on this brisk morning of December 9, 1531. He eats a breakfast of eggs, beans, and rice on a corn tortilla, and makes his winding way to the edges of the rolling scenery. As he approaches Tepeyac Hill, he begins to hear music.

Juan is a recent convert to Catholicism. Ten years earlier, Hernando Cortez took over Mexico City and ended the Aztec oppression of hundreds of thousands of human sacrifices. When Juan was just thirteen years old, he witnessed more than eighty thousand human sacrifices on top of a one-hundred-foot pyramid in just four days; Ahuitzotl, the Aztec ruler, took only fifteen seconds to remove the heart of each victim.

Now, as Juan draws closer to the music, he sees a brilliant light. He climbs until he reaches the top of the hill and sees the Virgin Mary standing in a radiant, heavenly glow. He listens as she tells him to go to the bishop in Mexico City, and instructs him to build a church where she is standing.

So he did.

Like Diego, I, too, journeyed deeper into my faith after seeing the hearts of thousands discarded. I also have had this particular relationship with the Virgin Mary—and by that, I mean talking with her.

We Catholics believe in something called the "communion of saints," which basically means that our death does not separate us from each other; and though we might not fully understand it, we know there is a heaven and that heaven is just another place where we are able to be in communion with each other. It's all about community. So, just as if I were to come to you and say, "My wife has cancer. Will you pray for my wife?" I can go to the angels and saints who are still *with* us, but are just in a different place. The beauty is that they are not even separated by a physical boundary. They are in their home of ultimate community.

In the simplest of terms, Mary is about communion through community, and community through connection. Mary's entire existence is about picking "the least of these" to be the mother of humanity—a thirteen-year-old girl who, under today's terms, would be snubbed or scoffed at. Her story is about bridging the gap between the divinity of God and the dignity of man.

A number of supposed apparitions have occurred throughout Christianity, where Mary appeared to people in different places, entering new spaces, and bridging these gaps for communion and community purposes. You may have heard about places like Fatima and Lourdes—locations of supposed apparitions where Mary appeared to the people of Portugal and France. Since 1981, Mary has been appearing in a place in Bosnia called Medjugorje, though it is not an approved apparition by the Roman Catholic Church (it takes more than a century to decide a thing like that).

Truth is, even if they say it's real, I am way more of a "Doubting Thomas" type than the guy who just buys into the whole deal hook, line, and sinker. However, there is something about Juan Diego and his vision of the Virgin Mary that resonates with me, something that feels particularly connected to my life and the lives of those explored in this book.

It turns out the bishop whom Juan Diego shared his vision with was a "Thomas" too. When Juan tells the bishop what he witnessed, the bishop tells Juan, not in so many words, "Baloney. I need something more than that."

So Juan goes back up and pretty much tells Mary (again, these are my words), "The bishop says, 'baloney.' He needs a sign to believe it."

And, boy, was he given a sign.

Suddenly, on top of the mountain, red roses bloom—during a time of the year when roses don't grow. Remember, it's mid-December. And, man, what a perfect symbol for Mary to give. Pain and beauty. How lucky for those thorns to have roses.

So Juan begins picking the roses and placing them in the *tilma* he's wearing, which is a piece of cloth made out of cactus fibers. He hauls a bunch of roses down to the bishop, unfolds the cloth, and, as the roses come pouring out, the tilma reveals a stunning image of the Virgin Mary.

Five hundred years later, you can see that same *tilma* framed in the Basilica of Our Lady of Guadalupe. People have researched this seamless garment and concluded that it's not a piece of man-made artwork, but, rather, a miraculous organic fabric that had somehow rooted in this pattern naturally and suddenly. No paint. There are stories of bombs exploding all around it during the revolution in Mexico City in the 1920s, but instead of harming the cloth, a cross that stood in front of it bent over, as if to take the blast. Just like that—a 90-degree bow—zero damage to the tilma, just as the cross has done for us. And, let me tell you, I've stood directly in front of that cross, only feet away, and have seen its powerful, unmistakable bow.

But I'm not asking you to believe any of this stuff.

I'm asking you to keep thinking about what the bishop's face must have looked like when he saw all those roses falling to the ground, and then fast-forward 475 years later to when a series of events brought me to the same location where this apparition occurred.

———

One hellishly hot day in March 2006, near Mexico City, I'm with a guy named Bill—a Catholic theologian buddy of mine pushing seventy years old—and we're making our way to a male convent in a little town called Tulpetlac. It's Lent at this Franciscan convent, and I'm sleeping on a concrete floor. This is like no place I have been before. If I want hot water, I plug this thing in the wall that is connected to tons of electrical wires hanging above a bucket of water, and it basically fries it hot. If I want to pee, it's into a hole in the ground. If I want food, it's the same meal every day, three times a day. That means rice, beans, scrambled eggs, and corn tortillas three meals a day. Everything is cooked in the morning and sits on a shelf the rest of the day. So when lunch comes around, as expected, you get your eggs, your beans, your rice, and your tortilla. But by dinner, the almost-day-old-egg deal is not quite working for me.

On day four, we get on this bus, ride even further outside the Mexico City metropolis, and are dropped off in the middle of nowhere.

Nowhere.

All there is to see is me, this balding, intellectual the-ologian, and two friars making our way to the Franciscan *Porziuncola*, a small church like the one in Italy where the young Francis of Assisi understood his calling and renounced the world he knew—a life of wealth and comfort—in order to live in poverty. After his death in 1226, they built around the chapel to protect this now-sacred place and later added a number of other huts and chapels for contemplative prayer.

And then there is the rose garden. This is where Saint Francis talked to the turtledoves, inviting them to praise the Lord. The story goes that one night Saint Francis felt tempted to abandon his new way of life, and so he rolled naked in the bramble thorns in an attempt to overcome doubt and tempta-tion. However, the moment his skin made contact, the bramble bushes turned into dog roses without thorns. Since then, these miraculous, thornless roses have grown in the garden.

What is it about roses? Is it that behind everything

beautiful there's pain? Is it that suffering and beauty cannot be separated? Are they synonymous?

All I know is that in this little Franciscan town, there were only unassuming chapels, huts, and rose gardens.

The upside? There are absolutely no distractions for anything *but* contemplative prayer. And, sure as hell, I contemplated.

We are walking, and walking, and walking, and I am *starving*. We pass nothing except the occasional little farmhouse, while keeping our eyes on the two Franciscan friars with their habits on in front of us, and, truth be told, I am feeling pretty cool. If you don't know what a religious habit is, it's one of those dark cloaks with a hood and a rope wrapped around the waist. The only problem with my contemplative state was that one thought would not leave my brain. I look at Bill and say, "Bill, you know what I want right now? I'd like a giant order of fajitas. I am starving to death."

We start laughing. But it turns out this contemplative desert scenery actually works—surely, this is why there was so much desert wandering in the Bible—and that silly thought starts to morph into a theology.

I want *meat*.

Now, maybe this thought is sounding a little too literal when it comes from a born-and-raised Texan who hasn't had barbecue in a week. But what I was thinking on that hot March day was that the church has lost its meat. I'm hungry. Our hunger for more—for love, for communion and community, for home—is much more difficult to remove than our hunger for bread. We need some meat. The gospel has gone vegan. (No offense to vegans—this is merely for purposes of analogy.) They just sling the Word out there and leave it for you to digest without the nutrients.

Thus, the *gospel con carne* was born.

Bill and I started to develop the theology of the gospel con carne, and that's the foundation of Mobile Loaves & Fishes. This organization took the gospel and put meat on it so that you and I can collectively partake in the gospel—so we can be prepared to go out and serve and our hearts can grow hardy.

It is about being filled with the heavy stuff. Truth is meaty. It's not so we can sit in fancy-schmancy churches that cost tens of millions of dollars, built by people who don't know how to go out and serve. The gospel con carne is the gospel of flesh and meat—of a reality that's gritty, and truthful, and of being embodied in flesh given a human form. The gospel con carne is about becoming fully human. However, it turns out that this isn't exclusively a modern-day concern:

> Though by this time you ought to be teachers, you need someone to teach you the elementary truths of God's word all over again. You need milk, not solid food! Anyone who lives on milk, being still an infant, is not acquainted with the teaching about righteousness. But solid food is for the mature, who by constant use have trained themselves to distinguish good from evil. (Hebrews 5:12–14, emphasis mine)

Needing "milk" indicates spiritual *infancy*. Spiritually, we look like babies still suckling at a mother's breast, unconcerned with the rich, hearty foods at the adults' table.

We are stunted. We are living cutlets at *best*. What then is the solution to this state of spiritual infancy? The believer in Christ is called to grow in order to be able to process and be nourished by "solid food" . . . the gospel con carne. The aim is to become well-acquainted with the person and perfect work of Jesus Christ.

To get stronger and start walking.

As we continue to walk in the desert of Mexico, we continue to develop this gospel, and we suddenly end up in this even *smaller* town. We go into the home of this impoverished family who happen to know the friars we're with. They welcome us inside and offer us a fresh glass of cantaloupe juice. Up until that point, I had never had cantaloupe juice, and, let me tell you, it is *mind-blowing.* When it hits my tongue, the flavor explodes with sweetness. But then I see a little girl who had been born eighteen months prior with the umbilical cord wrapped around her neck. She is a near vegetable. She is lying there, limp, staring off into the distance, and will never learn to walk, talk, or do anything. Her mother asks us to collectively pray over her.

I believe God can heal, but I have never seen *that* kind of healing. As I look at this small girl with her deep brown eyes glazed over, I am drawn into the drama of this intense situation.

Then they ask us if we'd like to stay for lunch.

"Um, yeah," we respond.

They bring out the *comal grande,* which is a giant, concave wokish-looking thing on legs. It has a place for firewood and a smoke stack. They light it up and slather oil on it. They throw on onions and some chunks of *nopales,* which are baby spineless cacti. They sprinkle some salt and pepper, and it was at this point that I began to salivate. I turn around and they have this *molcajete*, which is a volcanic rock bowl with a mortar and pestle, and they begin grinding serrano peppers and avocado. Then, here comes the meat. They throw on pounds of chorizo, and, as it hits, the smoke rises in clouds and into our nostrils. And then, more meat. They put down big slabs of ham and then start lining the outside with fresh, still-warm corn tortillas.

I have been to five-star restaurants all over the world, and I can honestly say that the meal I had in that tiny Mexican town was the most phenomenal gospel con carne I've ever had in my life.

And it was in one of the poorest homes I'd ever visited.

To get to that home, you had to make it your intent to put yourself there. It's not somewhere you end up while taking a jog in your Adidas shorts in your suburban neighborhood lined with fresh-cut grass and SUVs. The desire for meatiness often only comes when you're hungry; when you have a desire for more.

That's the key to the gospel con carne.

You've got to get outside of your comfort zone. You've got to go down to the places that allow you to connect with people. Encountering this hospitality—this Christlike hospitality in the poorest of people—is what you'll discover.

The poor of Mexico evangelized me. It's kind of a selfish spirituality—me wanting to be a part of their spirituality—because we all know the poor have an exclusive, special access to the gospel.

Here's the takeaway: We've got to change the lurking belief that any human life is more valuable than another. We must broaden the perimeters of our relationships and find a place for those left out. When we bear the beams of love, arms wide-open, we become more ourselves. We have to expect more for each other so that when we see Juan Diegos, we see impossibly red roses. When we see a child with glazed-over eyes and no movement, we see a family who fed the hungry with a true gospel con carne.

In the pages that follow, you'll encounter people whose poverty does not come from a lack of money, but, rather, from a lack of being loved. The greatest disease in the West is not contracting leprosy or the result of being strangled by an umbilical cord; it is being unwanted, unloved, and uncared for. America can cure or treat many physical diseases with medicine, but the only cure for loneliness, despair, and hopelessness is love. Millions of people across the world are dying for a piece of bread, but many, many more are dying for the smallest bit of love. For human contact. For *carne.*

This is a hunger for love. This is a hunger for God. These pages are filled with stories of smart, disappointed, and baffled people who, at some point in their lives, had no place to go nor people to go to. These are people with some of the best stories ever told, and their stories take time and effort to hear. I hope that by the end of this book your paradigm will shift, your eyes will open, your gospel will become meatier, and your love will grow greater. I hope that you will start to see the great "I AM" in the "least of these."[1]

Because, at the end of life, you will not be judged by how many dollars you had, how many friends you made, how many diplomas you earned, how many beautiful places you've seen, or thoughts you thought. You will be judged by "I was hungry and you gave me something to eat, I was thirsty and you gave me something to drink, I was a stranger and you invited me in" (Matthew 25:35).

Welcome homeless.

CHAPTER 1

THE THREAD, THE HEAD, AND THE HEART OF ALAN GRAHAM

THE WHOLE OF HUMAN LIFE IS MADE UP OF THREADS.

Together, human lives are woven into a fabric made stronger and more useful than its individual parts. But, isolated, each individual strand is more easily frayed, and unless other threads come together to be braided into a cord, the single strand will break on its own. When the threads of each individual life come together, they become a thing that derives its strength and resilience from the structured collection of its parts. And while our lives are made up of threads that seem disconnected, they are actually incredibly intertwined and tightly woven together.

The first intersection of threads in life is that strong, yet fragile, intertwining braid with the people who bring you into this world. That being said, the first and only memory I have of my parents together under the same roof as a married couple was when I was about four years old. My mom was standing on their bed with a knife in her hand, threatening my dad.

This took place in the master bedroom of a house in Bellaire, Texas, a suburb that's now been swallowed inside the city of Houston. This was a simple one-story home typical of those built in the suburbs in the early '50s, and at the time probably only cost about twelve thousand dollars. Like all childhoods, there are memories both sweet and sour, but this memory stands out because it is an origin story, a vivid depiction of our personal dysfunction. Mother needed help, but we didn't know that yet.

My dad worked for Humble Oil, which is ExxonMobil today. He was married to a stay-at-home mom who grew up in Wichita Falls. She aspired to be an actress and went west to California's famed Pasadena Playhouse, later crossing stage left to New York City. Things didn't work out on either coast, so she moved to Houston where she met my dad in 1950. My oldest brother was born in November 1951, and Mother told everyone he was born premature, coming in at just under eight and a half pounds. Funny. If you sit and do the math it just doesn't quite add up.

Eight years later, she was standing over my father, wielding a knife, and the next thing you know she's in the hospital. While she was admitted, she was subjected to some of the most powerful psychotropic drugs known to man. She was given electroshock therapy that froze her brain completely and unalterably. During these treatments, my father filed for divorce and unleashed an Armageddon of a custody battle for me and my brothers. He remarried pretty quickly, too, and as I look back, something was clearly going on while my mom was in the hospital. He was distracted and often unavailable, and, the truth is, I have always felt a bit sad for my dad. He missed out on so many memories—now stories that have filled the time I've shared with my own thirty-two-year-old marriage and four kids. I would have wished the same memories for him.

My maternal grandparents were well-off and opened their

purses like God opened the earth to swallow my father in the custody battle. They also were able to get their daughter some of the finest mental health care in the world, sending her to the famous Menninger Clinic in Topeka, Kansas, at that time, which gained its reputation as the leading intensive, individualized treatment for patients with complex symptoms. Think Marilyn Monroe and Judy Garland.

When she was released from the hospital, my brothers and I went with her. It's difficult enough for a single mom to raise a family, much less a single mom with an extreme mental health disability. By the time I was in the third grade, my mother— our caretaker and provider—was spinning out of control. She was hospitalized again, and off we went to live with my dad and stepmother, until another custody battle was fought, which Mom would win again.

She was probably hospitalized eight or nine times over long periods for the rest of her life. The drugs and the electroshock therapy began to take their toll. By the time I was in junior high, Mom was an embarrassment. My brothers and I didn't want to be around her. She had noticeable tics from the drugs' side effects, and as far as hygiene was concerned, she didn't give a crap. Poor Mom didn't have the capacity; when she would go deep into her psychosis, it was a total train wreck.

On Easter Sunday, March 29, 1970, I was fourteen years old. There were two tickets to see Led Zeppelin on my bedside table. This was during the Led Zeppelin II Tour, when I was (and continue to be) a huge Led Zeppelin fan. I was *stoked*. I was lying in bed when a knock came from the front door. I looked out the window of my second-story bedroom (by this time, we had moved from Bellaire to another area of Houston), and just beyond our mailbox were maybe three or four Houston Police Department cruisers parked out front. I knew they were looking for me, so I did what any kid would do. I hid in the closet.

As it turned out, this was not a very good hiding place, and I was promptly arrested.

During that time of my life, my friends and I would take cars and go on joyrides. The coup de grâce was when we decided to have a little destruction derby in a vacant field near our under-construction neighborhood. It seemed harmless, but deep down we knew we were being destructive. I have to admit, though, that to this day a little smile comes across my face thinking about those times. I remember sitting in the police station and saying to one of the officers, "If you wouldn't mind calling my mom, I've got these two tickets to see Led Zeppelin tonight, and I'd really love to go."

The officer laughed. Obviously.

It didn't really matter one way or the other. Mom was in no condition to come get me anyway. She was sitting in her own filth as I sat in the filth of thousands of miscreants, ne'er-do-wells, and the dregs of society just like me who had been left in the Harris County Juvenile Detention Center for Day One . . . Day Two . . . Day Five . . . Day Seven . . . Day Eight . . .

I finally came to the realization that no one was coming for me, except for maybe the transporter to take me to the Prison for Juvenile Delinquents in Gatesville. But there was an upside: my time spent inside those sad, gray, stark walls was pretty spiritual—as I sat there saying, *Come on, God; show up.*

Finally, my (biological) father showed up.

It turns out that he wanted me to marinate in that place before he got me out, but it was an important moment in my life—the moment when I began to see a pattern form in the tapestry of intertwining lives.

Let me just say that my dad was not a great father, and I feel sorry for him because he missed out on that. And though his coming did not fix or repair all that was going on in my life, it did straighten out the course enough for me to be where I am today. Whereas many of my friends would have—and *did*— end up on the streets. No mother or father got them out, and so, despite any possible fleeting poor choices or unfortunate circumstances, they became locked into that system. Meaning, they sat there until they were released onto the streets where they would stay because they had no place else to go.

They became homeless—physically, spiritually, emotionally, and psychologically.

The challenge—especially in dealing with such homelessness—is understanding. We have to recognize our own human weaknesses—our own fallibility. We have to realize that most of us are not *that* far from bankruptcy or foreclosure. Any of us could be laid off or suffer a sudden, debilitating injury. Any of us could be negatively affected by the lottery of birth, born into a dysfunctional household with no father to come and get us out of jail, or simply drew the short lot.

And then what? Where would we be?

But I digress.

Around the same time as my conditional conversion experience, my mother had one of her own. She became Roman Catholic. None of my siblings have any memory of going to church until this point, when she began to drag us to Mass, had us baptized, confirmed—all that religious stuff. I felt like I was the only one who wanted to go to church with her on

Sundays (at least that's how I remember it). For many years, she and I were the only ones to go to Mass, simply for our deep love for the church and its rituals, despite her unpredictable, crazy mental tendencies.

Maybe it was surprising that I eventually left it—like many do—but that love was deeply embedded into my DNA. Deep down, it was there. So, when I met my wife, Tricia, in the late 1980s, I considered returning. At that time, I couldn't care less about any "church." But Tricia was Catholic, so I kind of had to be in the church. At first we were the Christmas/Easter Catholics. Then I began to see Tricia taking the kids to Mass on Sundays, and it just looked like the train was leaving the station—so I made the decision to hitch my car to the family car. Now I had to endure the-kneel-and-stand-and-kneel-and-stand and so on part of Mass. But going through the motions yet again became another thread in my journey to where God was moving me, slowly, carefully, into these right places of *I am going to do something for you and with you, but it is going to come later.*

If you look over a lifetime, you begin to see these moments intertwine and think, *Where do I currently reside on this seamless garment that is being weaved? Which thread do I reside on?* I'm not sure how or why you have this book in your hands, but now that you do, our threads are crossing over one another, and we are connected, whether we're aware of it or not.

To be fully human and fully aware of this beautiful, seamless garment that is being woven, you must really discover who you are in Christ.

And who are you?

You are made in a very distinct image. You are a member

of the huge human family, where we're all brothers and sisters no matter where you come from, whatever your culture, your religion, or background. You were born in weakness, you will grow, and, eventually, you will die. Your story is the same as mine or anyone else's. It's a story of accepting that though we are a fragile individual thread, we are made stronger through our interaction with others. The mosaic that many of us call the body of Christ is incomplete unless there are no missing tiles; everyone is included. The banquet table of inclusion is infinite.

I see all these little moments along the way pushing me—all of these threads in this fabric pulling me. My mom's conversion. Her mental health issues. My walking away from the church. The reintroduction to God through my wife.

This kind of introspection isn't just how my mind works. Every single person in this whole world asks four questions: *Where am I? Who am I? What's wrong? What's the remedy?*

In other words: *How can I find a way through brokenness, chaos, and insecurity so that life can be secure and whole again? Where and how might I find a home?*

After a few years in the church, I began to build an intellectual relationship with God. I was studying everything I could about the Roman Catholic and the Protestant church, the Reformation, and more. I wanted to know everything so I could take the roots back to the cross. I had the head, but I didn't have the heart.

I went on a men's retreat called Christ Renews His Parish. Had I known going into it that we were going to hold hands and pray—God forbid, hug each other—I would not have gone. I never wanted *that* to be my spirituality. I spent the first few hours of a thirty-hour retreat feeling pretty uncomfortable, thinking, *How the hell can I get out of here?* I thought the retreat would be an opportunity to network with some medium-to-high net-worth Catholic guys, and maybe learn a little more about our faith. But, in reality, it wasn't that at all. After about four hours into it, however, I started thinking, *Maybe I'll put in another hour or two.* Before I knew it, it was one o'clock in the afternoon, and I was a spiritually broken man. For the first time in my life, I felt something inside of me—I thought, *Just say yes.*

Just say yes.

This moment was another pivotal moment of discovery in my design. This moment was the first turn of my spiritual rheostat knob. You know that little rotating, circular light-dimmer-switch knob most likely found on a wall in your house? The one you click on and the light is as dim as it can be, but as you turn the knob, the light becomes brighter? Anyway, on the "Alan Graham Wall" are two rheostat knobs. One is my professional rheostat, which, at this time, was high voltage—all the power and light was as strong and bright as it could be. Then there was the ministry light on the other side. When I clicked that one on, a dim light illuminated, and the other (the professional knob) dropped a notch. The diminution of the light was almost imperceptible, but, over time, those rheostats began to move in opposite directions. I think this moment at the retreat was when the movement was so great that you could discern the ministry light beginning to illuminate the room. It was a gradual process. But this was a big moment that led to a series of "just say yes" events.

I realized who I am through discovering the unity between my head and my heart. Through the head we are called to grow, to understand, and to work through things. But the heart is something completely, 100-percent different. The heart is a call for the concern of others.

This opened me up spiritually, making me susceptible to the opportunities that would unfold in the coming weeks. More so, this moment accentuated the fact that God equips the called, but He doesn't call the equipped.

As always, God would provide.

I don't know why, but I have consistently been called into leadership. I don't know if it's a selfish call, or if it just happened naturally, but I've always led—the German club, student council, football, stuff like that. So it's no surprise that I found myself acting as spiritual director to a group of men called CRHP (pronounced *chirp* and standing for Christ Renews His Parish) Team 10. At the same time, Catholic Charities was putting together something called the SACK (Social Assistance Christian Kitchen) Lunch Program. They were trying to bring together five cross-denominational churches to provide fifty sack lunches to the day-labor sites in downtown Austin. Of course, when my church came to me and asked me to lead that program, I just said yes.

I could see right off the bat that they needed leadership. I promptly took over.

Tricia and I organized all five churches, figured out all the health department requirements, decided how each church was going to be involved, scheduled what the menu was going to be every week, and organized and created a team structure where every night, five nights a week, volunteers would come make the lunches, which included two sandwiches, milk or juice, a boiled egg, a piece of fruit, a pack of cookies, and a prayer card inside a brown paper bag. The next day, somebody from that team would get them out of the refrigerator, haul them downtown, and bring back the empty crates.

The system was humming.

And then, sometime in the spring of 1998, my wife, our friend Mary Ann, and I had coffee together. Now, I maintain that we were having coffee at Jason's Deli, Tricia believes we were at home, and Mary Ann clearly remembers we were at church. Wherever it was (definitely Jason's Deli), this was the place I had the vision for what would later become Mobile Loaves & Fishes. And when Catholics have visions, the location where they have these visions becomes a pilgrimage site, and from that place comes holy water and medals and all kinds of spiritual craziness. It's funny, because this vision was planted in the brain of an inexperienced, unknowledgeable man with no real idea of how he was going to do it. This man also just so happened to be a Catholic *and* a serial entrepreneur—a recipe for never forgetting the vision.

Mary Ann was telling us about a ministry in Corpus Christi that pooled resources from multiple churches to give to the people who lived on the streets during the cold winter nights. As she spoke, the image of a catering truck entered my mind, bringing necessities from those of abundance to those who lack the most basic of human needs.

I didn't really know what a catering truck entailed. Remember, this is before the food-truck craze. I'd never eaten from a catering truck. I'd seen them. I'd gone so far as to make fun of them, calling them "roach coaches." Nonetheless, this idea of an effective yet affordable means of delivering food to the hungry would not go away. When I went to bed that night, it was still on my mind. I woke up the next morning knowing that we could franchise it and bring it to every church, every city, and every state to feed the homeless. (This is how entre-preneurs think: one truck becomes a thousand.)

Finally, after a couple of weeks of this idea not going away, I told Tricia about it. She just looked at me and said, "Oh geez, here we go again." (This is how the wife of an entrepreneur thinks: feast or famine.)

But she knew I was on point and that nothing could get me off it. I don't quit, even when facing the most difficult of circumstances.

There's no such thing as coincidence. There are no acci-dents in life. Everything that happens is the result of a calculated move that leads us to where we are. As G. K. Chesterton put it, coincidences are just "spiritual puns."[1]

When my spiritual rheostat turned at that first meeting, it allowed me to be susceptible to the opportunities that would open in the coming weeks. First, the Catholic Charities pro-gram that prepared me and planted a vision. And, finally, the moment of vision becoming reality—of abstract becoming actuality.

That moment: As the spiritual director, I took a group of thirty men on their journey. This journey included four men I was born to meet. These men would later become some of my greatest friends: Bruce Agness, Jack Selman, Mark White (a sociologist), and Pat Patterson.

Instead of men talking about hunting, fishing, and women, we talked about family and God. It's a relationship thing that none of us had ever experienced.

There was also another significant player.

Enter Houston Flake.

So then there were six. We called ourselves the "Six-Pack." There is much meaning in that term. You decipher.

Houston Flake was born in 1955 to a very poor mother and father who often were homeless. And Houston Flake, one of the smartest guys I knew, couldn't read.

But I didn't know that at the time.

Sunday morning, at the end of our weekend retreat, we came out with bags full of letters. We called them "HELP letters." As each man read his letters, we went through massive mountains of tissues. These grown men were bawling their eyes out because maybe a wife, a mother, a father, a brother, a sister, or people they didn't even know were praying for them, and they realized the enormity of the body of Christ, and this seamless woven fabric wrapping around them like a blanket.

Then, Houston got his bag of letters, and he couldn't . . . freakin' . . . read.

Shoot. What do we do?

We've got to get somebody to read these letters.

Well, Mark's a sociologist—let's get him to do it.

I've known Mark now for eighteen years, and he rarely talks. He is a great listener. Perhaps the best I have ever met. He's one of those therapists who just listens, and as he read the letters, we realized they were all from people in prison or kids who grew up on the streets. The letters were all about the amazing impact Houston—who himself had been in prison a couple of times—had made on their lives. Imagine, someone most of us considered part of the despised and outcast group, having such a profound impact on the lives of others in that caste system.

As I was listened to Mark read, I still had that vision of the "roach coach" in my head.

After the weekend was over, Bruce and I were hanging out in the parking lot talking. We wanted to continue the conversation—a conversation that in all reality had begun six months prior. You could even say it began the day I was born.

You see, Bruce was one of those threads that had crossed mine previosuly, but looking back, I knew it was all for this moment. When we'd first met at the retreat, we shared a little bit of backstory. *My name is Alan Graham. I was born in 1955. I've got this. I did that. I smoked dope. I snorted coke. I stole cars.* Whatever your story is, you have about twenty minutes to share it at the retreat. Well, in mine and Bruce's, we'd both come from Houston, we were both born around the same time, and we both went to Holy Ghost Catholic School when we were kids. It turned out that his mother was my third-grade teacher. And while we may not have met back then, our lives had paralleled and intersected, paralleled and intersected. We immediately bonded because we had such similar experiences.

And as we stood in the parking lot after the retreat, we were now close friends, and he was the first person (besides Tricia) with whom I shared my idea.

"What if we go out and buy a roach coach, fill it up with food, and drive around at night and serve the homeless?" I said.

He looked at me and said, "That's a phenomenal idea. I'll put five 'hun' in that deal." I responded with a matching five "hun." Generosity begets generosity.

He was my first investor, and we figured if we could pull together fifteen hundred bucks more we'd be able to buy a junker and polish it up. Sure enough, we shared the idea, and a couple other guys wanted in on the deal.

The roach coach idea was kind of happening, but it didn't take long for us to realize that we were just five white guys from Westlake (the highest economic zip code in Austin) thinking that we were going to go out and save the world and help homeless people.

We were clueless.

I don't know what it feels like to walk around all winter in wet shoes. I've never had trench foot. I've never had a skin infection that I couldn't get rid of. I don't know how it feels to hold a sign on a street corner for months at a time. I've never had to defend a grocery cart. My hands don't usually split and seep yellow.

I don't know real physical suffering. But I know a little.

Finally, we realized we needed Houston Flake.

We were meeting in a law office, sketching out the business plan that we'd present to the pastor of St. John Neumann to approve it as a ministry.

Not surprisingly, everyone was comfortable meeting at this location—an eleventh-floor conference room of whatever *hoorah,* ritzy downtown building that overlooks the capitol with a catered-in deli lunch. We had no idea that the only law office conference room that Houston had been in was some hole-in-the-wall court-appointed lawyer guy's office. During the meeting, we discussed what we wanted on the truck. One of us suggested phone cards (this was before cell phones were widely available)—*wouldn't that be awesome?*

Houston looked at us and said, "That is the dumbest idea on the face of the planet. They don't need phone cards. No one wants to talk to them. They don't want to talk to anybody. You need to put socks on that truck."

Turns out that to this day, the single most desired item on the trucks are socks.

After the meeting, Houston decided to take me to his own conference room.

We drove into South Austin and walked up a dirt path into the woods—grass growing high and filled with thorny stickers. Trash was strewn about here and there. About a hundred yards out, a woman sat in a chair drinking a beer, smoking a cigarette. The closer I got, the more stereotypically "homeless" the woman appeared. All of a sudden, I was absolutely, 100 percent in a space where I had no idea why I was there. I was a traveler in a foreign land.

As we approached, Houston said, "Hello, Marge. How are you doing today?"

She rose from the chair. He reached around, grabbed her, and pulled her in with this great bear hug. He had his hands on her shoulders and as he released the hug, he planted the sweetest platonic kiss on her lips.

I was looking at an ex-con, former heroin junkie, dope addict, alcoholic. And I was just this white guy from Westlake Hills. I knew I was about to be introduced to Marge, and I was going to have to shake her hand. I had no idea what was on that hand. Where had that hand been? What kind of cooties was I going to get off that deal? What disease might I contract? What was going to happen here?

What was happening was this: Christ had sent Houston to hold my hand and journey with me through this spiritual, stereotyping brick wall—slice through it like a stick of hot butter, and take me to the other side to the point where I could be soaked in urine and receive a big bear hug. Where I could learn to embrace the bouquet of Christ. The bouquet that more often smells of urine, feces, and days-old body odor than it does of freshly harvested roses.

Of all the people I have ever met in my life, in terms of who emulates Christ as I understood to be the Messiah, Houston Flake was number one.

In our culture we dress up these megachurch pastors in these little suits, with their "education" and their ability to vaguely pontificate, and we think those people best emulate the Jesus of today. Whereas the image of Jesus of today and tomorrow and yesterday is really the Houston Flakes—the broken and the battered, the Peters and the Pauls, the Thomases, the persecuted. Servitude that transcends. Not pastors in castles.

Jesus understood the connection between people was always meant to be relational, not transactional. In the beginning, it wasn't so much that there were plants and animals and no sin; it was that man had a deep connection with everything.

Think about it.

We are born into a relationship. You are born in the womb, deeply connected to and dependent on your mother. You eat what she eats. You hear what she hears. That need for connection doesn't change, but it can end up looking like a lot of different things. What gives consistency to people is a deep sense of worth—a feeling of being loved as we are loved by God.

So there's the head, where we are called to understand and to deepen the laws of the world, of nature, and so on. But there's also the heart. The heart is a very fragile part of us that allows us to feel connected to nature and tend to it.

So, to be fully human is tying together the heart and the head, and by doing this, we can be more aware of the threads that connect us.

You know that feeling of reading a book filled with dynamic characters who are so vivid and well-described, with so much backstory, that you feel like you know them? And when you finish the book you are a little sad to be leaving the story? Well, the world is filled with these stories, and all it takes is for you to just say *yes* to people.

To see people, we have to engage.

We have to get out of our cars and talk to people. To understand the street, we have to walk the street. To weave a tapestry, we have to first find the threads.

We have to see how others live.

Start seeing the world for what it really is—dirty, rough, tragic, and beautiful.

It is truly a wonderful mess.

This doesn't mean pulling up to a stoplight and talking to a guy every once and a while—learning his name and making yourself feel good. You can't drive away thinking, *Oh, poor thing.* You can't understand the heart of people from a car. You've got to get out of the car. You've got to crawl on your hands and knees. You've got to make desperate attempts to truly connect and learn someone's story. You've got to empathize, not sympathize.

Take that loose thread. Start to pull. Let the whole thing unravel. Let's start making something stronger. More beautiful.

Or you could just turn up your radio.

CHAPTER 2

HOUSTON FLAKE'S 400 POPSICLES

A DIRT ROAD SCROLLED BENEATH A PAIR OF OLD REEBOK TEN-nis shoes, one sole flapping between the pavement and the heel of a bare foot. The white line in the middle of the highway unrolled as the sky turned from moonlit to sunlit. Houston Flake had lost track of how many miles he'd walked, unsure of what town he was in or if he was even in California any-more. The lurching mountains left each valley a mystery, and, as the new day dawned, he hoped for more success—maybe a thumbs-up, a bottle of water, or a meal would allow for a few more miles than the day before.

As he reached the top of the hill, he saw a beacon. It was a billboard for a church with big, bold, black font against a stark white background that read: GOD WELCOMES YOU.

So Houston decided to walk the road leading to the church, hoping to feed his hungry stomach and perhaps panhandle a sandwich to take with him. The church was massive, but when he opened the big doors he found it empty. He walked alone through its maze of hallways filled with friendly verses about God's presence and Sunday school artwork with color-ful crayon depictions of Noah and his ark lining the walls. He occasionally begged the question, "Hello? Anyone here?" But it echoed, unanswered.

Finally, Houston stumbled upon the kitchen and opened the fully stocked fridge where he found some ingredients to make a baloney and Kraft American Singles sandwich. He thought for a minute and assumed no one would mind if he made a sandwich. There was plenty of food and it seemed like a welcoming church. He placed the Wonder Bread on a paper towel and then a jiggly-wiggly slice of circular "meat," and right as he unwrapped the plastic off the slice of orange-yellow cheese, he got caught. Within moments the church had called the cops and Houston Flake was arrested.

As Houston left the church and the man in blue opened the backseat of the cruiser, Houston remarked, in all of his sincere simplicity, "The sign said 'God Welcomes You' . . . so God must not be home right now."

—⁂—

Maybe God welcomes us, but perhaps we aren't welcoming Him, even in some of our church buildings.

The fact that a Walmart-like abundance in a church wasn't accessible to him, the poorest of the poor, did not mesh in his simple, uneducated mind. Besides, why would God welcome someone else and not him? To Houston, God was pretty simple, but somehow we've made God complex.

This is an important truth not many people think about. Simple, as a divine attribute, is the opposite of complex—meaning He is not made up of a lot of composite stuff. The simplicity of

God means God is not *made up* of goodness, mercy, justice, and authority. He *is* goodness, mercy, justice, and authority. Every attribute of God is identical with His essence.

God is light, love, and life. You don't think about the sun rising each day; it just does. You don't know why you love someone; you just do. You don't think about each breath you take; your heart just keeps beating.

This is how God is. He just is.

That's why Houston could be one of the smartest Christians I've ever met, even with no real ability to study the Bible. He understands the essence of who God is.

The most important text in the Bible for a straightforward understanding of God is Exodus 3:13–15. Here, God has just commanded Moses to go to Egypt and bring Israel out of captivity. Moses says to God:

> If I come to the people of Israel and say to them, "The God of your fathers has sent me to you," and they ask me, "What is his name?" What shall I say to them?' God said to Moses, "I AM WHO I AM." And he said, "Say this to the people of Israel, 'I AM has sent me to you.'" (Exodus 3:13–14 ESV)

God also said to Moses, "This is my name forever, and thus I am to be remembered throughout all generations" (v. 15). What does it mean when you ask your God, "Who are you?" and He answers, "I am WHO I am"?

First, I like to imagine God being slightly frustrated and, therefore, deciding to kind of screw with them. "Excuse Me? What does that even mean? I AM WHO I AM!" But in all seriousness, I can only imagine that in twenty-first-century America, God's shaking His head thinking, *Man, you all are way off.* God is not interested in our political agendas or our strategic evangelical gospels of attracting the masses. He is interested in being present and for us to want Him here. I think what He's thinking now is, *I am what I am and I'm not changing—so let Me know when you want Me as I am.*

Secondly, it means God is simple. He is unchanging. He is reality. He is forever. He is accessible. God is here on earth. I AM, here. It's time to accept Him as He *is* and have His presence make a real impact on our hearts, on our earth, and in our churches.

Think about it this way: "In the beginning was the Word, and the Word was with God" (John 1:1).

The Word is God.

So if God is, again, simple, then the Word is simple. Theological exploration and interpretation are all well and good, but they aren't 100 percent necessary to grasp who God is because the gospel can be understood by anyone, even the illiterate (maybe especially the illiterate). Everything that is in there is rooted in what you experience every day. I think it's how Houston didn't get bogged down in the legalities of the faith and believed it for what it was truly worth. He understood God as something that obviously exists and something he assumed would be in that church. His understanding of God was in his DNA; therefore, his "apologetics" were simple and utterly true.

I think people who are rooted in reality as it exists are going to have a better handle on what it means to love and understand God as the great I AM. He's not trying to dress up an untamable, uncontainable God in a fancy suit and tailor it according to how he wants to package Him. American physicist Charles Misner wrote an analysis of Albert Einstein a quarter century ago:

> I do see the design of the universe as essentially a religious question. That is, one should have some kind of respect and awe for the whole business. . . . It's very magnificent and shouldn't be taken for granted. In fact, I believe that is why Einstein had so little use for organized religion, although he strikes me as a basically very religious man. He must have looked at what the preachers said about God and felt that they were blaspheming. He had seen much more majesty than they had ever imagined, and they were just not talking about the real thing.[1]

Houston Flake had a mind more akin to the genius of Albert Einstein than most PhD-holding smarty-pants I know. How? A belief rooted in reality. A faith rooted in existence—living each day in the sun, in the cold, feeling the pangs of real-life hunger, weariness, and poverty—something many of us can't claim to have experienced. He had a creed rooted in what is, what was, what will be. His God was a God who should be welcomed in all places.

If we start thinking about the Bible as a memory aid, we can start living in reality. If we look outside a window and begin to remember why we're here and what we could be existing for, the Bible might actually mean something to us beyond a list of rights and wrongs, a historical textbook, or an opportunity to spit out verses like spitballs at whoever we perceive to be less adequate. If we look at the Bible as a memory aid meant to reorient us to where we came from and get us back home, it might mean we live a life filled with the kind of adventure it was always intended to hold.

At least that's what happened to me.

The moment Houston Flake became my tour guide was the moment I experienced full-on reality. It was life changing. It allowed me to have the kind of faith that doesn't ignore what's underneath the overpass, what's behind the back alley, or what's digging in the Dumpsters. It allowed me to know a God who doesn't pretend what's happening isn't happening but, rather, is in the Dumpster too. Most importantly, it allowed me to listen to what God is saying through what He places into my life and calls me to do.

There is a glorious whimsy of God, who temporarily places people into your life. To this day, I wonder what those people could have learned from Houston years ago in the kitchen of that church in California. What if they would have allowed him into their lives? Imagine what they could have learned. I know my life would look a lot different if I hadn't met him. It would look a lot worse. The moment Houston took me to his conference room changed my perspective on everything.

It went from my understanding of needing phone cards to needing socks—from stereotyping the homeless when going on our truck runs in the middle of the night, assuming that they would be up all night drinking and doing drugs, to realizing that, overwhelmingly, they are in bed at 8:00 or 9:00 at night, just like most of us who aren't homeless. They are eating their food at dinnertime. Imagine that. It was a major paradigm shift for me. Houston allowed me to realize that we just had to drive into the middle of town to feed someone, as opposed to going to a hobo camp by the railroad tracks or the dark recesses of alleys. Another paradigm shift. After the first truck stop with Houston, I no longer needed him as a tour guide. It didn't take him long to teach me the obvious, simple truths that for some reason hadn't occurred to me before.

Right after that first truck run with Houston, people started recognizing the truck, and the food and materials it provided became a lifeline. I would look in my side-view mirrors and would see people running behind the truck in the middle of traffic, waving and yelling, "Stop! Stop!" That's when I equipped each truck with JPS technology: Jesus Positioning System.

Those trucks have itineraries. According to our schedule it needed to be on the corner of Lamar and Riverside at 5:00 p.m. and then down in Zilker Park by 6:00 p.m.—but if you are driving from one stop to another stop and someone flags you down, you're likely being called to that person at that particular moment. Many, many stories have unfolded from that philosophy. You begin to realize the power of that truck being visible and out on the street. It allows you to randomly and providentially meet strangers who you wouldn't have encountered if you had only been herding them to a street corner at each designated stop.

It was also important that we didn't hand food out from above, from inside the truck, but rather on the ground, on the same side of the truck, guiding the hungry through their options—and, yes, there are options. The element of choice plays an important role. Having the choice between a meat

25

and cheese or a PB&J, Fritos or Cheetos, Snickers or snicker-doodles, orange or apple, milk, juice, water, or coffee, are the little bitty choices that people who live a life in extreme poverty don't often get to make.

These trucks don't look like your average soup kitchens. The soup kitchen flowed out of the philosophy of scarcity that originated during the Great Depression, where you had to throw a couple of rocks in some boiling water with salt and pepper. In the 1930s there was genuine scarcity. There was no food. There was no money. Fast-forward to today and we live in the most abundant country in the world. We live in a country of accessibility where, for most of us, what we need is minutes away, even if it's just going to a 7-Eleven. You walk inside and there is an assault of food options, and, yet, if you walk into a modern-day soup kitchen, it's still rock soup.

God calls us into this life of abundance. God *is* abundance. Trust me, He didn't give us an array of vegetables for us to be stuck with just celery. He wants us all to partake in the whole chef's salad.

But if God is abundance, what does it mean if a guy walks into a church and asks, "God is here?" only to conclude, "Nah, God isn't in here."

It means the church is delusional. It means the church has become a me-first, isolationist environment. We think mega-churches mean we've got mega-believers; but what it really means is we're getting a lot of soft, biblical vegetarians who can't digest the meat and think that it's okay to believe in an I-AM-WHAT-YOU-WANT-ME-TO-BE God. But when you really start breaking down the numbers, you'll see that mega-churches are resulting in a huge number of mega-churchless.

The number of adults in the mainline Protestant churches decreased from about forty-one million in 2007 to thirty-six million in 2014, according to the Pew Research Center.

Exacerbated by its decades-long protection of sexual predators within the priesthood, the Catholic Church has also lost three million members over the last decade—its hold on the U.S. population falling from 24 percent to 21 percent.[2] Combine that information with the fact that the average age of the congregant is fifty-two, and you've got to ask yourself, *What's going to happen in forty or so years when the average congregant is dead?*

But I think it'll be alright because there will always be tour guides like Houston Flake. There will always be the janitor at the church, making eight bucks an hour, whom the majority will disregard but whom Christ will deliberately put in our lives to bring light to what is true. He'll teach us that the real-life God is irresistible and the poor are the *point* of the church. When I count my blessings, they start with Houston Flake.

Our relationship, however, was cut short according to my human timeline. I'm sure the providential timeline had other things in mind.

Houston suddenly contracted bladder cancer and was given a death sentence of a few weeks left to live. So we asked him, "Houston, what's your dying wish?"

Paris? Disney World? An African safari? A fine bottle of red wine and a big steak dinner?

Nope. Not Houston.

All he wanted, when given the choice, was to hand out four hundred popsicles to the children who lived in the Meadowbrook Housing Projects in South Austin. He wanted to give these kids the kind of thing they didn't often receive. He wanted them to choose: Pink? Red? Blue? Purple? Green? He wanted to give that which they did not need but might want. He wanted to give them abundance in fruity, tasty, frozen form.

When he became hospitalized, he was unable to go to the housing projects. So we brought the popsicles to him in a truck that was newly dedicated and had inscribed in big, bold, black font against a stark white background: "In Honor of Houston Flake." We wheeled Houston outside in his hospital gown, cart dangling with bags of liquid and IVs stuck in his toothpick arms. His gaunt face smiled and laughed as we rolled him over to the side of the truck carrying ice chests filled with popsicles.

We passed them out to the children and anyone else who wanted them on that hot July day. We had a blast handing out the little plastic tubes of joy, and this opened up a whole new world of beauty. My own self-important impediments were swept aside, and it turned into an authentic self-forgetfulness through something as small and silly as pull-apart popsicles. This self-forgetfulness is the number one thing Houston taught me—a profound education from the uneducated. I got a lesson of abundance from the impoverished. The same guy who taught me to give people what they need (socks) also taught me to give people what they want (popsicles).

Sometimes you think you're going to be the guy to save everyone by feeding people, but then you realize that those people are going to save you.

As Houston looked at the truck, he said something to me that resonated so deeply it reverberated throughout my body and still reverberates to this day. In his somewhat broken, uneducated English, he said, "I don't think nobody's ever honored me before."

My heart sank. I can't even go a day without somebody patting me on the back or someone saying what a great job I've done. Houston went a lifetime. I don't know what kind of impact that has on a human—to never get even the tiniest bit of approval.

So we made a plaque that had a picture of the Six-Pack—the founders of Mobile Loaves & Fishes—which included Houston Flake. We attached it to the front of the first truck, and underneath the picture we engraved, "In Honor of Houston Flake."

I'm embarrassed to say that when the plaque arrived it sat in my passenger seat for days. Houston had moved into hospice and everyday I'd look at it and think, *Man, I really need to take that to Houston before he's gone.* And every day it'd get away from me.

Finally, I grabbed my oldest son, Decker, and we went to the hospice center where Houston was. When I went to the front desk, I said, "I'm here to see Houston Flake."

She pointed. "His room is right over there." I went to the room, looked in, and came back out. My heart was pounding hard.

"He's not in his room," I said.

"Well, he might be on his patio smoking a cigarette."

So I went out to the patio and he wasn't there either. My heart was thudding back and forth on what felt like my back and chest. My whole body was beginning to sweat. I rushed out to the parking lot and walked around, then I heard someone yell, "Hey, Alan!"

There was Houston sitting in a car parallel parked along

the street behind the building. As I walked toward him, the sweet aroma of marijuana entered my nostrils, and I saw that he was sharing a joint with his daughter. We talked for a while, and I gave him the plaque. He cried. I cried.

And then just like that, three days later, he died.

My time knowing Houston was short. He came into my life, moved all the furniture around, forced me to relearn what I thought I already knew, and then he left. This homeless-pot-smoking-cussing-street-guy better demonstrated the characteristics of Christ than anyone I had ever met up until that point. His thread was interwoven with mine to make this incredible pattern, and then it just stopped.

—ᚱ—

Our lives are threads. The overlapped weavings are where relationships are found. Relationships are where human life flourishes.

Human connections are as important to our survival and flourishing as the need for food, safety, and shelter. They teach us how to live. They make our lives more colorful. But over the last fifty years, while society has been growing more and more prosperous and individualistic, our social connections have been dissolving, our threads have grown thinner, and the tapestry of our lives appears more dull.

We volunteer less. We entertain guests at our homes less. We are getting married less. We are having fewer children. And we have fewer and fewer close friends with whom we share the intimate details of our lives. We are increasingly denying our need for human connection at a great price. Over the same period of time that isolation has increased, our level of happiness has gone down. Suicide rates and depression have multiplied.

Across the board people are sacrificing relationships for the pursuit of cash. The American Freshman Survey has tracked the values of college students since the mid-1960s. This survey is a good measurement of how culture and our priorities change over time. In 1965 college freshmen said that "starting a family" and "helping others" were more important than being "very well-off financially." By the 1980s it was the opposite: "helping others" and "starting a family" were less important to college freshmen than making a lot of money. In 2012 that number peaked to 81 percent as freshmen prioritized being "very well-off financially" more than anything else.[3] It's a not-so-slow spike.

Now *that's* baloney.

But, hey, I'm optimistic. I think deep down we all know that a pursuit of money over a pursuit of people is not how we were intended to live. I think it's just another lesson we need to learn from the Houston Flakes of the world. I think that we are eventually going to look down and see ourselves as living jiggly-wiggly sliced meat paste and decide we want something meatier. Something substantial. We're going to want to stop being little mushed meat in plastic casing and start taking on the bodies we were given.

The cerebrum is the largest part of the human brain that handles the high brain function stuff like thought and action. It controls your voluntary muscles—the ones that move when you want them to.[4] You hear that? Thought *and* action. You aren't designed to just think about it. You're designed to act on that thought.

You aren't designed to look at someone and think, *Who can I pass you off to in order to get you what it is you need?* You shouldn't call the nonprofit, and you certainly shouldn't call the cops. You can't expect the guy behind you to be able to spare the change. You are designed to be aware that life is bringing this person to you right now for a reason. What are you going to do? Here you are right now—what can you do to help this person? How do you stay in this person's life long-term? If you want to experience reality the way it exists, you've got to jump in.

Look around at the people in the room where you are sitting and allow yourself to be impacted by their existence. Don't just people-watch. What good is watching? We can't keep watching things. We've got to be *seeing*. Our homeless brothers and sisters are making it easy on us. They wave and hold signs and share their story on the flat side of perforated cardboard. More often than not they're already telling us where their home is. They're standing on the street corner, welcoming you inside.

Houston didn't make it so easy. We were clueless he was homeless until God put him in our lives and wove our lives together without our even knowing it. It was a slow process that mulled and brewed and boiled and sat. When I zoom out, I see that all along my life was leading up to Houston and that Houston was going to lead me to more.

More friends.

More family.

More stories.

More lessons.

More life.

Thank God for this providential tour guide who took me by the hand and guided me through the adventure of a lifetime.

CHAPTER 3

DUMPSTER DIVING
WITH J. P. BURRIS

HOW MANY MOO COWS YOU THINK HAD TO DIE FOR THAT YOUNG lady's jacket?" He pointed to a young dark-haired waitress wearing a light brown jacket that was (1) probably fake and in reality made of polyester, and (2) worn by a waitress in her late twenties who was not likely the root of all his frustration. But his frustration, anger, and annoyance knew no discrimination.

"Besides, what's the point of a fancy jacket like that? God don't see ya with clothes on. He sees you buck naked. He sees you stripped down to your bare ass the way you entered this world—cause that's the same goddam way y'gonna leave." He's wearing a blue bandanna around his head, faded old Levi's, and a black long-sleeved shirt under a holey T-shirt that says "Keep Austin Spicy." I think he could be the sole source of Austin's spiciness.

But inside the rough and spicy exterior is a truly soft and sweet heart.

J. P. Burris lives alone in an RV in East Austin. Leading up to his home is a mosaic trail made of a number of found materials—glass, brick, tile, stone, wood—and this short little trail is outlined with pink and white petunias, a crystal-looking glass elephant, a sign that says "Everybody's Somebody," and a variety of porcelain angels that were either discovered in someone's trash or given to him by a little neighbor girl who would trade J. P. a stolen angel for a story. Also on his lawn is a grocery store cart (likely his most valuable tool), an old ramshackle dresser, a picnic bench, and tangled Christmas lights that cover his RV and spill over onto the cold, hard ground. Currently, his trailer is dark with little furniture but a bed. You can also see carpentry tools scattered on the floor—dark and gray but oddly meticulous. He leaves his door open as he shuffles some things around. When he arrives back in the frame of the shadowed doorway, he's holding the single most beautiful thing I have ever laid my eyes on.

It is golden against the dirty whitish RV and seems to illuminate despite the surrounding darkness. It looks both ancient and new, surpassing time and space, memory and the present moment. Looking at it reminds you of that part of the movie where everything suddenly makes sense and everything is wholly explained because of this one little seemingly insignificant object. It's like *Citizen Kane*'s Rosebud.

J. P. is holding up a small wooden rocking horse. Twenty-three years ago, before everything fell apart, J. P. took his two-year-old daughter on a horse ride. They shared a horse, and she sat right in front of him as he held the reins tight and his daughter tighter. When they got home that evening, little Bobby Joe asked her father for a horse. Desperate to figure out a way to give his little girl what she wanted, he racked his brain for a way to get the money for a horse. At that time he was still doing the garbage truck circuit, known as the only guy on the crew who would take two trash cans at a time and dump them into the truck—sometimes weighing a hundred pounds each, over and over and over again. No one surpasses J. P. in his work ethic (and, I'd argue, strength).

Realizing that buying a horse for his daughter was a mere pipe dream, he went to the dump and found old fence posts and wood scraps, and he formed them together into a small rocking horse fit for a two-year-old queen. She dragged and rode it everywhere on the concrete floor of their house, and it withstood the hardness of the ground. She slept beside it because where she went, the horse went.

Until one day when J. P. got home to find all of his things a pile of ash.

This was caused by the official signing of the divorce papers the day before. The only thing his wife didn't set fire to, protected, I assume, by his daughter's affection for it, was the wooden rocking horse. Bobby Joe had outgrown it, so he left his home with nothing but a wooden horse.

This is when things were no longer maintained.

J. P. relapsed and became newly addicted to cocaine. He had struggled with drugs, heavy drinking, and pornography before, but cocaine took it to a whole other level.

His father was a Native American in the army, who fought in World War II, the Korean War, and Vietnam. Native

Americans can't be drafted, so J. P.'s father had to volunteer. He obtained two Purple Hearts and the right to brag about crushing and killing hundreds of German soldiers under his tanks. I've never killed anyone before, so I'm not quite sure what it would do to my psyche. But what it seemed to have done to J. P.'s father was make him a hard, dysfunctional man. I guess one's sense of humor becomes twisted because, somehow, this man found it funny to get his four-year-old son drunk in front of his friends for a good laugh. Through experiences like that was how J. P. came to know the world, so it's no wonder he was more susceptible to addiction and more desirable of numbness. He eventually moved into his grandmother's house but, in his words, "was likely to give her a heart attack because I was such a dumbass." So he moved into the children's home, and picked up odd jobs here and there. As a child he worked as a roofer, and then he worked for twenty years as a garbage man. He also worked several years as a car washer and several more as a heavy-equipment operator. Now he makes his money by scavenging and Dumpster diving, all the while just barely able to keep his head above water. He is an incredible scavenger, finding the oddest little things and treasuring them and giving away the things worth nothing but sentimentality.

But he makes most of his money through paper and aluminum collection. One party on fraternity row on the University of Texas campus—known fondly as "The Snake"—can produce a harvest of hundreds of pounds of Keystone Light cans alone (and about a hundred ping-pong balls). Unfortunately, that only amounts to maybe fifteen dollars after pushing it five miles down Congress Avenue to the metal yard.

———~~~———

I met J. P. in the summer of 2003, during what we at Mobile Loaves & Fishes call a "Street Retreat." It was a totally unstructured retreat that only became that way once we realized the true silliness of preparation—of cute little binders with discussion questions and pulled scriptures, and filled with answers to practical questions like, *How many pairs of underwear should we bring? Are pillows allowed?* Why on earth (literally) did I ever think for a split second that experiencing life on the streets would be structured? The only way for a purely transformative and powerful experience to take place, and for the Holy Spirit and the human narrative to move through you, would be to go out and live without shelter and without worldly possessions for forty-eight hours. It was like getting into the icy cold river of life in an inner tube with no boat rudder or engine pulling us. The river just takes us where it goes. That is what the Street Retreat is about. Where are we going to go?

But with this question comes hesitation.

There is usually a great deal of fear and trepidation in people's lives leading up to the retreat—the fear of the unknown. The fear of *Am I going to get attacked or raped by a gang of marauding homeless people?* And battling those fears is virtually impossible. I can't take that fear away. Fear is what keeps us from loving God with all our heart and all our soul and loving our neighbors as ourselves. Fear is primarily self-generated. The closer you are to Christ in the grand scheme of things, the closer you want to be to Him. It's not that I want to die right now, but paradise? I wouldn't turn it down. But almost always after the first fifteen to thirty seconds of being out on the streets, we are going, *Huh? Why was I feeling that way?*

This is a way for people to journey much closer to Christ. We become closer when we become intimate. We're usually isolated. We wake up in the morning, and the TV is on. We're pelted with the bad news du jour, and then we crawl into our dark garages and our dark cars. The doors lock behind us, we push a button, the garage door opens, we back out, we close the garage door, and we essentially drive safely and securely until we get inside our covered parking garages. We then make our way to our covered cubicles, and we think that we've surrounded ourselves with all of this safety, but, in reality, we've just built up all this fear. I believe that nothing new is going on today that hasn't been going on since the advent of man. Violence is no more, no less. We just see it a lot more because it is available to us with all of our communication mediums. So we live in this fear. One of our fears is homeless people. Walking around downtown and going to a restaurant is totally acceptable behavior at 7:00 or 8:00 at night, but if we are going on a Street Retreat to hang out with homeless people, at exactly the same time, in exactly those same addresses, it's deemed unsafe.

What happens if we throw away that fear? We'll realize how intimate we can become with the Creator, and we'll end up wanting more of that intimacy. That's where the power lies.

For this Street Retreat, fifteen of us were dropped off in Wooldridge Park—our clothes still clean, hair still combed, socks still white and sitting high on our ankles, backpacks sealed tight, and probably looking like tourists. Imagine how hilariously idiotic we might've looked to the locals, let alone to true street folk.

Enter J. P. He came swaggering in with unadulterated suspicion. "What do you yahoos think you are doing out here?" he asked, surveying the obvious. "You guys aren't homeless." He continued to look around, still trying to get a handle on what we were doing. I was there with my oldest son, Decker, who at the time was only fifteen. Both he and I were enamored with J. P. "You yahoos want to go Dumpster diving with me to see how life on the streets *really* is?"

Obviously, I had no desire to eat out of any stinking Dumpster, but before I could utter my gut reaction of "Hell no," Decker piped out a boisterous "YES!" So myself, Decker, and another retreater, John, took off to East Austin from downtown at about 8:00 or 9:00 p.m. to pick up J. P.'s buggy—an HEB grocery cart hidden in the bushes. You see, HEB, which, for all you non-Texans, stands for Howard Edward Butt, is the most widely accessible grocery store in Texas and has the best and strongest carts for this type of work. They are large, metal carts unlike Target's red plastic carts or Whole Foods' small, two-layer carts.

There, in the bushy backwoods of quick-to-gentrify East Austin, J. P. welcomed us into his humble abode and introduced us to his dearest friend—a real, live fox that lived in a den nearby. We grabbed his cart and began to push this HEB mobile in a serpentine manner from East Austin through downtown and into the state office building district, stopping at Dumpsters all along the way and jumping in and out to harvest recyclables. By 2:00 a.m. we had collected around five hundred pounds. Pushing the buggy up and down the hilly streets of downtown Austin was not an easy task.

The next morning the fifteen of us met back up, and we looked at each other in utter amazement, each experiencing life on the streets differently and each experiencing not only the Holy Spirit, but also our fellow man in totally different ways. *You're not going to believe what happened to me last night.* And our stories kept unfolding and unfolding.

The next day, myself, Decker, and John were sitting in the gazebo in Wooldridge Park with another homeless guy, also named John. We were just chatting about this and that when John #1 pointed to John #2's backpack and asked him where he kept the rest of his stuff.

"Well," John #2 responded, "what stuff?"

John #1 followed up, "All your possessions?"

Then John #2 held up his bag and said, "Right here is everything that belongs to me and everything that I need." This unfolded a dialogue about what it would look like if we had to stuff all of our things in a backpack and carry it around—your house, your car, your insurance policies, all of your furniture—imagine carrying that around on your back. What would it look like if we drew a picture where the imagery was that you carried everything that you owned? You'd be flattened. It's an extraordinary burden to which we pay a lot of attention. That in and of itself separates us from God. Whereas this guy, John #2, had nothing and there were no impediments. He's not lying around at 1:00 a.m., perusing Amazon trying to figure out what he needs to purchase to get delivered by a particular date. Having all that stuff is an impediment through attachment. We think that by living a certain dream there's hope in that. There's no hope in that. We came into this world buck naked, and we're going out the same way.

———m———

While walking around on the retreat, J. P. showed me an orange tree downtown. It was seemingly public property, where he would get a bit more nutrition than what he would normally get from the soup kitchen. One day, someone had chopped down the tree. There didn't appear to be a reason. It was a beautiful tree in the park that gave fruit and had the added bonus of aiding in someone's well-being and potential survival. I seriously hope I am wrong, but I can only assume that the city considered J. P. (and people like him) an inconvenience, so they turned a tree into a stump. Why is it that so many of us would cut off our nose to spite our face? Why on earth would someone cut down a tree, something that inherently is not our own, preventing someone else from enjoying its fruit?

While some people fail to see the value of a bright, juicy, vitamin C-jacked, nutritional orange, J. P., on the other hand, won't let an acorn fall outside of his attention. A moment together hadn't passed without him saying, cigarette dangling out of his crusty mouth, "Hold on, ya yahoo, follow me." He'd stretch his neck above any visual obstructions, peering just beyond, and shuffle in and out of cars, commenting on some terrible restoration of a turquoise-and-white 1955 Ford Fairlane, and he'd jump over curbs and grassy medians to a tree. He'd look up and then down on the ground, saying, "Dangit. I swore there would be acorns around here."

J. P. was nuts for nuts. Nuts were his way of giving back. He would take two toothpicks, break them each in half for limbs, and stick them into the shell of the acorn. Then he'd draw on little eyes and a smile to make an acorn doll. It was something he enjoyed doing as a kid.

There is another fond memory he has as a child. He says it's his favorite memory. His uncle would get a walnut, take out a Swiss Army knife to cut it in half, remove the meat, and replace it with a ten-dollar bill for J. P.'s stocking at Christmastime. J. P. believed that magic like that could only come from Santa Claus, only to grow up and realize that he, too, could be the source of such magic.

So now, he scours for walnuts and hides little rings and coins and trinkets, for kids and adults alike, blessing everyone with one of his few warm childhood memories. He's always showing me the things he finds and can't believe that people throw out. Today it is a small wooden box that he has refurbished. Something someone spent money on and that someone threw away. Disposed of. Worthless. Old made new.

As J. P. would say, "Chicken poop into chicken soup."

Sometimes when we dive into the chicken poop, it's not pleasant. A lot of times we will just want to bail. J. P. sued me twice and threatened to do so many other times. One time, he even sued me for five dollars because of a broken propane tank. I ended up giving him twenty bucks just to not deal with a lawsuit. It was one of those times my brain just wanted to place J. P. in a box with "Pain in the Ass" written in bold, black Sharpie across the top of it. (Don't worry, I'm sure he'd put me in a similar box in his mind.) He does things that I cannot begin to wrap my mind around. But his existence has brought so much joy and awareness into my life that it totally outweighs the frustration.

I don't need full clarity on why that is. I don't think we have to enter into relationships with the need to fully clarify why that relationship exists. Our brains perpetually seem to go into a "DTR" mode. In our determination to define the relationship, we say "work friend," "mentor," "girlfriend," "boyfriend," or "college friend," and we bind people by where they exist and how they served us for a season. But the truth is that with a brain of all-inclusiveness, the need to understand and constantly DTR goes out the window.

J. P. is my brother, and, being the scavenger that he is, he found a bunch of beautiful six-inch nails. He shined them and painted them and offered the idea to send them to our sponsors and donors along with beautiful borderline poetry.

Help us nail down our future by making old things new and broken things work.

Aren't nails, like thorns, the starting point of restoration and rebuilding? Isn't that where this all begins? The nails driven through mesial nerves are the very nails that restored and rebuilt us.

It was in looking at J. P.'s keen sense and ability for restoration that I began to see that Christ's life, death, and resurrection was being applied to a truly cosmic restoration that would eventually culminate in "all things new" (Revelation 21:5 ESV). Even the smallest wooden box with an elephant on the lid had the capability of being cared for. Someone designed that elephant. Someone cut that wood. Someone, in some way, placed the design on the wood and sold it for however much. Someone bought it, and my money is on the fact that someone gave it as a gift. Then someone threw it away.

J. P. is the one who saved it.

He is the one who spent the time cleaning it and refurbishing it and making it new. Even old thrown-away fence posts and splinter-ridden stakes in the ground can bring immense and unfathomable joy to a daughter and her father.

He asked me if the glass-plastic-poly-whatever elephant in his yard was crystal. It wasn't, but I still replied, "Yeah, maybe." He said, "Screw you, I know it is." This small ability to see the potential renewal in anything and value in everything, so embedded in J. P., brought a new sense of sacredness to all space and all practice, as everything was now seen on a heaven-bound trajectory of restoration.

I woke up to the story of "all things new" during that Street Retreat, and the reality of it began to surface in some remarkable ways. It seems that the promise of "all the ends of the earth shall remember and turn to the LORD" (Psalm 22:27 ESV) is being fulfilled. There apparently is a deep story we are capable of remembering if we look toward our memory aid.

J. P. embodies Christ's most creative trait and the gospel's most epic ending. The gospel is the ultimate story that shows strength coming out of weakness, life coming out of death, and rescue coming from abandonment. And since it is a true story, it gives us hope because we know that life is really like that. We see it in Christ, and we see it in J. P. Burris.

CHAPTER 4

DANNY HENDERSON'S STREET NAME IS PREACHER

THE HEAVENLY PATRON OF ALL EXILES—OF THOSE WHO WERE ripped from their place of dwelling and left floating, half-person, half-something entirely different—is Danny Henderson.

It was 1988 and Danny had a pretty successful carpet and upholstery business in Los Angeles. He remembers to this day a particular job in Beverly Hills—one that earned him five hundred bucks in one day. It was a huge house; the owner was some president of a major Tokyo bank, and, in that moment, ol' Danny thought about how things were going pretty well. Business was good with a set of solid employees, a home, a wife, a six-year-old girl, and a four-year-old boy.

But, as they often do, things fell apart. His wife took off with another man and Danny's two children, leaving him with a 1978 Kingswood station wagon and a business that was going under. He liquidated everything to pay off some debts and began sleeping in his car with only twelve hundred dollars in cash that would—over the course of four months—diminish to twelve dollars and thirteen cents.

With that much to his name, Danny was driving down Long

Beach Boulevard when his car broke down. That moment would mark the beginning of his twenty-seven-years-and-counting stint on the streets.

He hadn't been on the streets before, so this was a pretty terrifying moment. He had been living in the car for a while, but the difference between a car and a sidewalk is that you can lock the doors of a car. When someone sees the car as a target for burglary, they leave you and it alone once they see you sleeping inside. Danny stepped out of the car knowing he would leave it there to finally be impounded. Cars were whizzing past, and it was in these freshly fragile instants that he suddenly ached for his children. He was desperate for his old job. Before even one night on the streets, he was dying for his old life. He packed everything he could carry into two heavy trash bags, including some tools, extra clothes, and a Bible, and began leapfrogging the bags down the highway, picking up one and carrying it a hundred feet and then going back for the other and carrying it two hundred feet and so on. Back and forth. Back and forth. His clenched fingers, wrapped in the thin, white, stretchy bag, turned the plastic from finger molds to holes. He had no idea where he was going or where he was going to sleep. He was a Vietnam vet, Special Operations, 83rd Airborne, did POW camp raids as a part of an extraction team, and, still, he was more afraid being on the streets than he ever was in Vietnam. At least he was trained for what he did over there. He wasn't trained for what was about to happen on the streets. He wasn't trained to deal with what he found when he turned the corner into an alleyway lined with repulsive junkies, prostitutes, and rats.

Unable to empathize or imagine this new lifestyle, he

thought, *My God, I'm not like these people. I am not lazy. I just want to find some work. This will pass.* But the recovered addict in him was particularly susceptible after this sudden, profound, catastrophic loss of family, and it didn't take long for him to assimilate. He quickly discovered that a lot of these people weren't addicts when they became homeless. A lot of these people weren't alcoholics when their wives left. A lot of these people weren't prostitutes before they were raped. What Danny discovered was that more than 70 percent weren't addicts until *after* they had been on the streets for about four to six months.

This was when Danny, totally alone and isolated, fell fast and hard into a life of gambling to fund a cocaine addiction. His grandmother, a woman who raised her four siblings at the age of twelve when her parents left, was constantly bailing him out so he wouldn't end up like the Cuban refugee in the corner of the alley who had whip marks on his back, healthy teeth ripped out, and scars where those who needed payment had burned him electrically. Danny did his best to make money to survive and pay his grandparents back. The only thing he ever stole was a squeegee from a gas station. He found a bucket in the garbage, cleaned it, filled it with water, and moved on to the gas station next door, running up to any car that pulled in asking, "Can I wash your windows for some spare change? Just trying to get something to eat."

Sometimes he'd make a quarter or two. Sometimes he would get five-dollar bills and his eyes would bulge. One time he got a twenty, and he nearly passed out. He'd make his way around independently owned burger stands, Chinese food stops, and fast food restaurants, asking if anybody wanted their floors mopped, their trash emptied, or their parking lots cleared of litter—anything that could be done in exchange for a good meal. Many obliged and some of them even sent him on his way with a little bit of cash in his pocket. One of them had him clean off caked garbage, a quarter-inch thick, from the walls of trash cans. It was gunky and disgusting, and Danny, like anyone would, fought back the urge to puke.

He would find bags of old donuts behind the donut shop, each donut smashed up against another with five different kinds of topping—a glazed, strawberry, powdered sugar donut with maple icing and coconut shavings. He ate so many hodgepodge donuts that to this day he can't eat another.

There was a moment when Danny thought he'd figured it out. He remembered back to when he owned his business, and he worked with guys who wanted to start their own businesses. He'd move around their schedules to provide them more flexibility as they established their own clients and built up the funds for their own equipment for carpet cleaning. When they left, he wasn't bitter, but was proud of their hard work. So, naturally, Danny thought, *Of course they will give me a job after everything I did for them.* But when he went to meet them, they saw his deteriorating appearance and denied him work. Their excuse? His missing teeth and extra facial hair might not look good for their new company's image.

The reality that they wouldn't do what he had done for them when he was hungry, *hurt.*

I think it's true that if you get hungry enough, you just start eating your own heart, because the truth was that when he did have any cash, no matter how much time had passed since he last ate, he would spend it on drugs—self-inflicted punishment for the way things were going. People who have not dealt with addiction don't understand it; people who have dealt with addiction don't understand it.

So, for empathy's sake, let's try a little role-play.

For a moment, imagine you're one of the rats chilling with Danny and your other rat pals one evening in an alleyway.

You've got beady red eyes, a long thick tail, and little rat claws. People don't like you much other than to use you for experiments; and, lucky you, you're chosen for one!

One day, you're ripped away from all your rat friends, and they put you in a cage all by your lonesome and you've got nothing to do but eat the same ol' brown pellets, drink some plain ol' H_2O, and sleep on dry wood chips, and every few days a giant human hand comes along and gives you more food and then you just eat, drink, and sleep. One of those days, a giant human hand puts another bottle right next to your water bottle, except this new liquid in the new bottle makes you feel kind of different. It's kind of exciting. It breaks up your day a little bit. You're a rat, so you don't know why this water is different—it just kind of makes you feel funny—which is a refreshing thing for water to do if you are isolated and alone all day, every day.

Now imagine you aren't in a cage but in a rat park two hundred times the floor area of the other cage. There are at least twenty other rats, both male and female, a variety of food, colorful balls and wheels for play, and enough space for mating. There are two bottles, one with plain pure water and one with this other water—the water that makes you feel kind of funny. But you've got so much fun stuff to do that the funny water isn't really as attractive anymore. The feeling it gives isn't worth it because it takes away from your time playing and eating with the other rats.

The key ingredient in the funny water was dope, and the rats in isolated cages drank nearly nineteen times more morphine than those in the rat park.

This was an experiment conducted in the late 1970s by Canadian psychologist Bruce K. Alexander. It showed some evidence for the effect that community, abundance, and love have on addiction.

In one of the experiments, Alexander forced rats in ordinary lab cages to consume the morphine-laced solution for fifty-seven days without any other liquid to drink. When they moved the rats into the rat park, they were allowed to choose between the morphine solution and plain water.

When given the choice in the little rat village, the rats exclusively drank the plain water despite showing some signs of withdrawal.[1]

Now, one thing I'm sure we can all agree on is that man is *slightly* more emotionally complex than a rat. So what does that mean for man's feeling of alienation, particularly when we live in such an impersonal society? It is worse when a man can exist on a crowded street and still feel like he is in a solitary rat cage, totally alone. I find it so strange that someone without blankets and a sleeping bag is just somebody up early in the morning, sitting on a park bench. But someone with a sleeping bag is *nobody* up early, sitting on a park bench. The first guy you don't mind sitting next to. The latter you keep a good hundred feet from.

This is what happened to Danny Henderson.

But here's the key: just like the rats, Danny's drug use drastically reduced when he was introduced to some friends who demonstrated love, abundance, and affection. Once he moved to the place he would stay for almost three years near a river on Lakewood Boulevard, he met Randy and Beverly, two other homeless people near his camp.

Danny was the new guy in the camp with the moaning stomach. Randy and Beverly had gone to the supermarket—jumped in the Dumpster, found lettuce and tomatoes and bread, and bought a big bag of potato chips and one or two liters of fruit punch. Beverly shoplifted some cheese, lunch meat, mayonnaise, and mustard, and when they came back with this feast in hand, the two introduced themselves to Danny and handed him a paper plate with a big layered sandwich, chips, and a cup of fruit punch. When he finished eating, they asked if he wanted another one. *Had he had enough? Is there anything more he might want?*

This moment was the turning point that eventually led to Danny's total sobriety. Imagine that. Just a pinch of kindness. Just some garbage lettuce and a bit of turkey and Swiss cheese. And one cup of Hawaiian Punch.

They didn't know him, but they helped him. To this day, if you ask Danny, they were the ones who had the greatest impact on his entire perspective on giving. It was then that he began regularly spending his last dollars on a taco for his neighbor or a bagel for a stranger. He eventually gave this act of giving a name—a ministry called Up From the Ashes, taken from 1 Samuel 2:8: "He raises the poor from the dust and lifts the needy from the ash heap."

This is how Danny picked up his street name, Preacher.

This guy who never had more than twenty bucks in his pocket would take people out to eat. His favorite place to take them was Spires, an old diner, where he would sit across from them as they looked at the menu, scanning the laminated page for the cheapest thing—like a cheeseburger, knowing that Danny was in the same place they were. He'd snatch the menu out of their hands and tell them that if they were just going to pick the cheapest thing off the menu, he would have to pick something for them.

Sure, his funds were limited, but if he didn't have enough to take them out to eat, he said he'd let them know. He wasn't interested in going the economy route. What he wanted to do was give them a good meal and hear their story.

Danny was now sober and shaven and clean. He'd use the gas station nearby with an outdoor bathroom (which is almost impossible to find these days). As a result of his clean disposition and his upward attitude, people saw something different in Danny. He would tell them his story, his journey toward recovery, and his belief that everyone had a God-given purpose, including them. Across the table, Danny would watch as tears made clean tracks down their faces, dripping off their chins, and dropping into little mud puddles on their plates.

He started doing this whenever he had any money, and it's this generous spirit that inspires me most about Danny. He is the single most generous man I've ever met. He is also the most content. So that's why our truck runs are not a feeding ministry. The truck runs use food as leverage to connect human to human, heart to heart. And, sure enough, that's how I met Danny. I was on a truck run back in 2010, and he got a peanut butter and jelly sandwich and my phone number.

Eventually, Danny found out where his children were. His son, only sixteen years old, was in a maximum security prison.

His daughter, nineteen, was still in the care of her foster parents and had been molested for years by the man that Danny's ex-wife had left him for.

———w———

In June 2010 Danny left me a voice mail asking if Mobile Loaves had any discounts with Greyhound. We didn't, so I bought Danny a ticket to Minneapolis so he could celebrate Father's Day for the first time in twenty-two years. To make it in time, Danny left on a Thursday, only to find out on that very same Thursday his son had violated parole and was back in prison. Danny was able to visit his son by participating in what they call a "video visit"—only able to see him on a TV screen. His daughter gave him a phone call because her foster parents didn't want her to see him for reasons still unknown. That was his long-awaited, long-anticipated Father's Day. But at least it was more than he'd had in twenty-two years, or since.

I asked Danny if we could have coffee when he got back. That was when he told me his story, his thoughts and ideas, summarizing his philosophy by quoting the parable of the separation of goats and sheep in Matthew 25:32–33, 41–45.

> All the nations will be gathered before him, and he will separate the people one from another as a shepherd separates the sheep from the goats. He will put the sheep on his right and the goats on his left.
>
> Then he will say to those on his left, "Depart from me, you who are cursed, into the eternal fire prepared for the devil and his angels. For I was hungry and you gave

me nothing to eat, I was thirsty and you gave me nothing to drink, I was a stranger and you did not invite me in, I needed clothes and you did not clothe me, I was sick and in prison and you did not look after me."

They also will answer, "Lord, when did we see you hungry or thirsty or a stranger or needing clothes or sick or in prison, and did not help you?"

He will reply, "Truly I tell you, whatever you did not do for one of the least of these, you did not do for me."

Danny is one of those who is "blessed by my Father" (v. 34).

Danny not only represents the least of these—the least of what society has to offer—but he is also somebody whose tithes are 100 percent. Danny taught me what this parable truly means. He, more than anyone else, taught me what it means to be blessed.

Let's break down the seven things that separate the sheep from the goats (also known as the seven corporal works of mercy). These are taken from the Roman Catholic Canon and are just as much commandments as the infamous ten.

1. Feed the hungry.
2. Give drink to the thirsty.
3. Clothe the naked.
4. Shelter the homeless.
5. Visit the sick.
6. Visit the imprisoned.
7. Bury the dead.[2]

This is what Christ observes on Judgment Day. For most of us it's going to be a longer list of what we didn't do than what we did do. Notice it doesn't say, "Feed the hungry, unless you think he might just have the munchies, otherwise let him starve." Or, "Clothe the naked, unless he doth get drunk on Jack Daniel's." Or, "Bury the dead, unless you think the dead guy doesn't have any friends or family." Or, "Visit the imprisoned, unless he was imprisoned for holding up a 7-Eleven. In which case let him rot in jail."

Danny didn't care if he took them to Taco Bell while they were tweaking. He just wanted to make sure they had a full stomach, felt loved, and, in that same moment, had a conversation to help them understand that their God would want them to eat and feel loved as well—that they, too, will be blessed in the kingdom of heaven.

And here's the key problem with the prosperity gospel and using the word *blessed* when we have a cushier bank account than someone else: It alludes that "they" are not blessed. *The Lord has blessed me but not them.* I can't tell you how many rich people I've met who are positively miserable, and that amount of money plus that amount of sadness does not a blessed man make. Somehow, *blessed* is being used when *lucky* is the right word. That's some twisted Mad Lib. Our memorized response to material bestowals is to call ourselves *blessed*. On the surface the phrase seems harmless. Why wouldn't I want to give God the glory? Isn't that the good thing to do?

If we're looking for the definition of *blessing*, Jesus spells it out pretty clearly in Matthew 5:3–12:

> Blessed are the poor in spirit, for theirs is the kingdom
> of heaven.
> Blessed are those who mourn, for they will be comforted.

Blessed are the meek, for they will inherit the earth.

Blessed are those who hunger and thirst after righteousness, for they will be filled.

Blessed are the merciful, for they shall be shown mercy.

Blessed are the pure in heart, for they will see God.

Blessed are the peacemakers, for they will be called children of God.

Blessed are those who are persecuted because of righteousness, for theirs is the kingdom of heaven.

Blessed are you when people insult you, persecute you and falsely say all kinds of evil against you because of me.

Rejoice and be glad, because great is your reward in heaven, for in the same way they persecuted the prophets who were before you.

So why would someone think that God has blessed them more than Danny because they have a nice car? The truth is that there is no earthly or spiritual reason why one person has more than some other guy because it is beyond comprehension. God doesn't give people things because they are *more* Christian, *more* loved, or because their prayers were made in perfect King James Version English. It's great that one person has a comfortable life filled with lots of fancy resources (and, of course, that person should indeed be thankful and thank God for these helpful resources and bonus gifts), but I do not think for one second that God's going to call that person more blessed.

He might, however, call that person burdened.

In many ways the guy who has all these resources is, frankly, burdened by them. Remember the guy who carried a toothbrush and clothes in his backpack because that was all he had, versus the imagery of another more materially well-off person carrying everything he had on his back? Squished. As they say, mo' money, mo' problems. When my new Apple Watch starts wonking out, I've got to pencil in a time in my busy schedule to go to the Genius Bar at the Apple Store. (Yeah, I have an Apple Watch, and I love it.) We all know vacations are one of the most stressful things—money, packing, making sure the whole family is happy. My bet is the guy who is stripped of all these resources probably has a closer relationship with God because instead of dealing with all these problems, he is able to talk with God. All the material stuff we have—the office building, the vacations, the car, the house, the pretty clothes and such—can be an impediment to our relationship with God. This is just the truth. *You will know the truth, and the truth will set you free* (John 8:32).

The other and more serious reason that our idea of blessing is terribly offtrack is based on the notion that if you're hoarding all your resources, you've got some serious 'splainin' to do.

God's going to ask what we did with all that money. What did we do with all that time? What did we do with all that treasure?

I equate time, talent, and treasure to the Father, the Son, and the Holy Spirit in three persons. No one can separate them. No one can say, "I give my time, but I don't give my treasure." We have to give all three because, like the Trinity, they are inextricable. It's the trinity of stewardship. We have to live our lives well in order to be spiritually connected to the Creator. To be a steward is understanding that all we are and all we have is a gratuitous, undeserved gift from God. I didn't work for this. I was just in the right place at the right time. I am a dropout from the University of Texas. I couldn't even make it in school. Sure, I've worked hard, but I've also been in that place where it was just given to me. If all that we are and all that we have is an undeserved gift from God, what do we do to show our gratitude in return? Is it the 10 percent tithing thing?

The spiritual thing to do is recognize where all our bonus resources are coming from. What are we going to do to make sure someone is warm tonight? That someone won't go hungry?

How much is enough when it comes to giving?

Enough is all, but it's pretty hard to do.

Even Mother Teresa struggled with her chocolate fetish. Man, she loved chocolate. So whenever she got a gift, it was chocolate.

While in Calcutta, India, Mother Teresa was planning a trip to Ethiopia, and the children of Calcutta—who were in poverty beyond any Westerner's understanding—asked her if the children in Ethiopia were in need. These children—beggars, ragpickers, and laborers—gave Mother Teresa any money that they could find to give to the children of Ethiopia. Of course, the donations were no more than a penny per child, but they were given at a great cost and sacrifice. Whatever they had, they gave. A little boy then approached her crying, and said, "I have nothing. I have no money. I have nothing. But I have this piece of chocolate. Take that and give it to the children in Ethiopia."[3]

Mother Teresa, who told this story at the United Nations, said, "That little child loved with great love, because I think that was the first time he had a piece of chocolate in his hand. And he gave it. He gave it with joy to share, to remove a little [of] the suffering of someone . . . this is joy of loving: to give until it hurts."[4]

After that experience, Mother Teresa gave away chocolate as a sign of her love.

How much love do we put into giving?

The *Didache*, a late first-century book that acted kind of like a manual on how to live, said it like this:

> Give without hesitating and without grumbling, and you will see whose generosity will reward you. Never turn away the needy; share all your possessions with your brother, and do not claim anything is your own. If you and he are joint participants in things immortal, how much more so in things that are mortal?[5]

Goodness.

I'd go back and read that if I were you.

We are united, each of us, in the love of God. We are family—brothers and sisters made in the image of our Father. To love is to bless and be blessed.

This is why Danny Henderson is a blessed man. He may live in a dump in the woods, but he certainly has a lot of wisdom. He has a close relationship with man and God, and he gives until it hurts. But, then, he gives so much beyond that it starts to feel good again. Danny is a content guy because he is living out his purpose of furthering the kingdom on earth, by giving everything he's got.

For some of us that might look like making a whole lot of money and then redistributing it to those in need. But we are fooling ourselves in thinking that we can ingratiate ourselves beyond anything humanly reasonable. When you think of what is being peddled to Americans today, we are constantly thinking of things to sell to each other. There are stores dedicated to dogs and cats. Not just feed stores, but manicures and pedicures for our pets, and day care for our pets. But then we can walk down the street and step over people who may be dying.

G. K. Chesterton helped come up with the idea of *distributism*, an economic ideology upon the principles of Catholic social teaching. This concept encourages us to reach the point where our basic needs for happiness are met—food and shelter—and then we ought to work our heinies off in order to lift other people to that same level of happiness. So if you are a hundred thousandaire, use your hundreds of thousands of dollars to help other people. If you are a millionaire, use your millions to help other people.

This isn't a government model. It's a spiritual model telling us we should be giving 50 percent, 60 percent, 70 percent, or 80 percent of our income to help other people. Plenty of people could easily and happily live off of 20 percent of their income. If someone has fifty billion dollars and gives twenty-five billion away, I'm sorry, I will not stand up and applaud. I will, however, applaud a man with twelve dollars who spends 90 percent of his total net worth on pancakes for a stranger.

Preacher is one of those rare kinds of religious leaders who actually offers up everything he has so others can be lifted up. If you give Danny a hundred-dollar bill, he will buy fresh socks, fill them with ten-dollar bills, and place them in the tents of the homeless. During the Austin floods in the summer of 2015, he stood for days on the street and raised two thousand dollars, which he then gave away to his homeless brothers and sisters to purchase dry sleeping bags, tents, and food. I still don't know where or on what he slept during that time, but my bet is it wasn't much, and whatever was there was wet.

He taught me that everyone has his or her own specific

purpose in life, and to feel and live out that divine purpose is enough. Love's enough. No one can be replaced. No life can be repeated.

Is Preacher *really* homeless?

I don't like calling Danny homeless because so much about him is so *homeful*. Especially when so many people with extraordinary homes are pretty homeless when it comes to matters of the heart and soul.

One thing I consistently see in my friends without a roof over their heads is a better understanding of what it *does* mean to be home. They have a better understanding of what it means to give. It's this unique, kind purpose and *homefulness* that has allowed Danny to be the brilliant brainchild behind some of the most innovative ideas we use in our organization today.

The first idea was H.E.R.O. (Homeless Emergency Response Operation). Danny thought it would be a good idea during disasters, like floods, to have homeless guys trained and knowledgeable of where camps are located go help their brothers and sisters through the disasters. These guys take tarps and tools into the campsites and act us their insurance, their FEMA. Because when the homeless get wiped out, it's apparently okay for them to be wiped out. But wouldn't they be thrilled to get a few days in a hotel or motel?

I have picked people off the streets on the coldest nights of the year—particularly on the lookout for raging alcoholics, because their chances of dying are much higher due to the fact that their blood is much thinner. I've tried taking people to nice hotels downtown, but the management will widen their eyes and ask us to leave. So we'll drop them off in pigsty hotels instead, and these formerly-on-the-brink-of-death men and women will begin to cry and thank us.

More recently, a truck team launched out of the commissary called Truck Team 888. The volunteers—made up of formerly or currently chronically homeless men and women—go out with food and meet the homeless where they are. Truck Team 888 helped solve a lot of the problems of not being able to reveal where all of the campsites are to volunteers or indicate where the locations of the truck stops will be on a Web site.

This is why Danny says he *prefers* to be the least of these. He likes to be at the bottom because he looks forward to his place on the right side of Christ along with the sheep, rather than the goats. Danny is homeless in the same way Jesus was homeless. Just because Jesus was a vagabond who consistently gave God 100 percent, not a mere 10 percent, and walked around with little change in his pocket, did not mean that He was homeless. He knew his home more than anyone who has ever existed in the world. Ultimate *homefulness*. Truly blessed.

—∾—

One evening, Danny was making his way back to his three-foot-tall dinky dome tent and was looking for a cigarette. He stopped by Claire's tent, a friend of his. He thought maybe she was still up even though he didn't see a light inside. So he asked, "Claire, y'home?"

Well, she wasn't thrilled to be woken up, so Danny went back to his tent and went to sleep. Then, a few hours later, around 5:00 a.m., a shrill and raspy voice awoke him screaming, "DAN! DAN! WAKE UP, DAN! HOW DO YOU LIKE IT, DAN?! WAKE UP, DAN! ARE YOU AWAKE?"

"Yes, Claire. I'm awake."

"Good. I'm glad to hear it, Dan. Have a wonderful day. I'm going back to sleep. *Don't* bother me."

Danny took a few deep breaths, and about ten minutes later he made his way back to her tent.

"Claire?"

"Are you serious? What do you want now?"

"You hungry?"

"Yeah, so what? I ain't got no money."

"I'll buy breakfast. Let's go to Denny's."

"Huh? Are you for real?"

"Yeah, on me. Let's go."

"Give me five minutes."

They went to Denny's and had the Grand Slam for $2.49, five coffee refills, and a glass of orange juice. Sure, there were some duct-taped rips in the vinyl seats and the sun had yet to rise, leaving that creepy-but-oh-so-charming fluorescent lighting that all decent diners have, but the bacon was crisp, and the pancakes are available 24–7.

Denny's was Danny's key to get to know Claire, and that was Claire's key to beginning her recovery. She would eventually go on to lead addiction meetings at one of the most renowned recovery programs in one of the largest churches in America. All for $2.49. That may not seem like much to us, but at that moment it was everything, and it was enough to open the door to a relationship that changed a life. This is what the power of abundance can do. Even the poor in pocket can be rich in spirit with pancakes and a side of bacon and eggs.

Grand Slam indeed.

CHAPTER 5

PEGGY AND DAVID: THE BABY BOOMERS

ON A BALMY SUMMER DAY IN EAST TEXAS IN 1958, TEN-YEAR-old David Shiflet was feeling ballsy. He and his friend were on their way to the pasture and had decided to leave their shoes at home because sometimes you just have to take off your shoes and feel it all. Even the bad stuff. When you're young and the weather is just right, the thorns and rocks and mud are no match for your ambition for adventure. The combination of ambition and a BB gun could only lead to an inability to withstand one more day of using mere aluminum cans as a target.

Their dirty little feet carried them far as they looked for something to spark inspiration, when, suddenly, they saw it. This colossal thing standing a few feet in front of them—just beyond the fence. Something so big and epic that it would indeed make this day stand out from all the days leading up to it. This would be the day that would make David a man.

It was a bull's behind. And, as you probably know, a bull is the male counterpart to a cow. And what does a bull have that a cow doesn't? Well, it's likely the same thing that David didn't have until this very moment.

The two young (soon-to-be) men jumped the barbed-wire fence for closer range and squatted low in the tall grass. They rested the guns on their shoulders, left arm slightly forward with the finger on the trigger, and one squished-shut eyelid per boy. They simultaneously pointed, aimed, and—*pew!* Bull's-eye. The back-to-back thud of the BB pellets making impact was followed by a gentle swing of the two dangling "things." They started to laugh and high-five each other, and before they even had a chance to look up, the bull was making direct eye contact while making his way to David. They hightailed it out of there, and by the time they got to the other side of the fence, the bottoms of their feet were scraped and bloody. Once they made it home, out of breath but satisfied, they each washed their feet with the hose in the front yard.

———※———

About four years later and a couple hundred miles southwest in Round Rock, Texas, Peggy was born. It was the 1960s, so it was perfect timing for the approval of a drug called thalidomide—one that promised to ease nerves, rid morning sickness, and thwart miscarriages. But it resulted in a legion of baby boomers born without limbs, hands, fingers, and toes. This was, of course, before the concept of "diversity," and so hundreds of children would forever live on the fringe of society. Even peer-reviewed medical journals referred to these infants as "monsters"—as if they were responsible for their own deformities.

Mothers even disowned their sons and daughters.

Peggy was one of those daughters.

Her mother rejected her before she was old enough to

understand things like "deformity." Peggy was born with feet but no legs, and with hands but no arms. She was regularly beaten for the way she looked. She was moved to the second floor of her mother's house, and her chair was taken away, leaving her to squirm on the floor. I'm still not sure whether or not Peggy was given her name out of some sick joke. Throughout the world about ten thousand cases were reported of infants with deformities due to thalidomide; 40 percent of thalidomide victims died before their first birthday.[1] This disaster prompted a lawsuit that required the German drugmaker to make payments to the survivors. But Peggy's mother stole whatever money Peggy received from the lawsuit so she could buy brand-new cars for the whole family at the expense of leaving her daughter homeless. With the help of her brother, Peggy got out of there as soon as she could and escaped to the streets. She eventually found comfort and numbness in methamphetamine and crack cocaine.

Around this same time the creation of a psychoanalysis method was introduced by D. W. Winnicott. He divided the world not into regular people and monsters, but rather into one kind of person with two senses of identity: the "True Self" and the "False Self."

You see, this guy saw the True Self as being rooted in infancy and the mere experience of being alive—blood pumping, lungs breathing, heart beating—prior to any sense of judgments, when everything is new and refreshingly and exhaustingly beautiful. Out of this comes a sense of what's real and a sense that life is worth living. The baby's spontaneous gestures come from instinct and, if responded to by the mother, become the basis for the continuing development of the True Self. Ideally, a continuation of finding life worth living.[2]

However, when parenting suffers, the child's True Self is affected. Instead, the kid tries to become what the parents or others want him or her to be. The result is the creation of the False Self, where "other people's expectations can become of overriding importance, overlaying or contradicting the original sense of self, the one connected to the very roots of one's being." The danger is that "through this False Self, the infant builds up a false set of relationships, and by means of introjections even attains a show of being real," while, in reality, they are just concealing a deep emptiness with an I-am-independent facade.[3]

Peggy's mother wanted her to have arms and legs, but Peggy couldn't *grow* arms or legs. So Peggy never knew what she was truly born to be—in a world with spontaneous open gestures, motherly love, and freedom from judgment. Rather than feeling a sense that life was worth living, she wanted to feel nothing at all, and the numbing from the drugs helped.

Though one might think that Peggy never really got the opportunity to meet her True Self due to such an unloving mother and poor science, the truth is that her identity was more rooted in reality than that of the majority of Americans. For others who desire the material, we're defined by big homes and a sense of independence. Defined by the fight to the top and self-serving attitudes. So we create division and are threatened by anyone who has desires different from our own—because they must be monsters, right? To choose a life on the streets? What's up with that?

In 2003 I was grabbing a taco at a local spot down the street from the office when this couple came over and accosted me, telling me they recognized me from the newspapers. They told me they like to meet interesting people but have no real interest in helping people who "just need to get a job." Well, as it turned out, they did, in fact, know a lot of interesting people because this couple happened to own one of the most fancy-schmancy architecture firms in the city. They build multimillion-dollar homes for the rich and famous. We continued to talk, and I invited them on a truck run to deliver some bagged lunches.

The first time is always the same, hesitant with this righteous sense of obligation—*Sure, I should do some good; just need to make sure and bring my hand sanitizer*—and within no time they're in tears and emotionally wrecked enough that they decide to do it a few more times.

But this couple was somehow totally different than the norm.

When the truck parked the two of them witnessed hundreds of weary men, women, and children come out of the woods. Many of them came eagerly, yet gently and slowly, to receive their peanut butter and jelly sandwiches. Mr. Architecture Man sat in the truck thinking about the last time he did some good, and his heart made fatal impact with the thought that he could not remember when that was. For fifty-five years the only person he had helped was himself. For years he had built twenty-million-dollar homes for people who were unhappy with the size of their Jacuzzi tubs, when these homeless people in front of him now expressed genuine and immense joy from a boiled egg and a fresh pair of socks.

This guy's name was David Shiflet, and *this* was the day that made David Shiflet a man. The old David had died, and a new David was born. A true David.

He saw one particular guy with a missing arm and a cannonball-sized dent in his head.

"Alan, what can Mobile Loaves do to help this guy?"

Wrong question.

"Nah, man. The question is: What can David Shiflet do to help this guy?"

This was the instant David was hit by the realization that you can't just expect the next guy to take care of it. You can't sit at the red light and expect the guy in the white Suburban behind you to be the one with spare change. Based on this realization David helped "that guy" and then an additional five people. More importantly, six incredibly deep friendships were formed and a rare understanding of what it means to really love was achieved. He realized that there are no coincidental encounters—instead, God places certain people in your way very intentionally.

—⁓—

A year has passed since David's first truck run. It was now a brutally cold and rainy night on the corner of South Congress and Ben White Boulevard. Peggy, now about fifty years old, sat in her electric wheelchair, worrying that the rain might blow a fuse and fry the whole thing, leaving her immobile. In her opinion, the best scenario would be for the thing to fry *her* so she wouldn't have to go through with the decision she had just made for herself. Unable to take the cold any longer, she decided that either tonight or tomorrow, she would ride her chair in front of an 18-wheeler on Highway 290. But for the time being, she sits there in her usual garb—a long skirt pulled up to her armpits, unable to wear a jacket and unable to afford a blanket.

A normal night for Peggy is devoid of any semblance to the actual meaning of the word *normal*. Most nights she attempts to find solace under the awning of a 7-Eleven in order to charge her wheelchair, but she's regularly kicked out by management. "Get your ass out of here! You can't charge that damn thing for free." She rolls away fearful on a regular basis. Men come and dump her out of her chair and onto the ground, lift up her skirt and rape her, sometimes putting her back in her chair and other times just leaving her on the ground. This makes her feel more like a semen receptacle than a human being.

The same night I decided to pick up some folks off the street to get them out of the 21-degree weather and into some hotel rooms, so I called David and his wife, Kay, who were more than happy to come along with me. When we discovered Peggy, David and Kay put her in a hotel for two weeks. They later discovered it had been more than nine years since this woman had slept in a bed—nine years since she had slept horizontally. She had spent every night for nine years in her chair, or awake and fearful on the ground until someone helped her.

So David and Kay bought her an RV and a cell phone upon which she recorded the voice mail greeting: "Hi. It's Special P. Talk to me."

This was the first time in Peggy's life she felt safe. Things that we often take for granted, like doors and locks, are revolutionary for Peggy. She walked into her new home to find a more functional and hospitable bed, a new computer, a "grabber" in order to get things off of a shelf, and a fridge stocked to the brim with Diet Coke—an addiction David and Kay decided to fund.

Now imagine the life Peggy could have had all along had

it started out with this kind of love. How could one ever get a job when they can't even clean themselves after they use the bathroom? Someone would have to do it for her.

—⁂—

On Maundy Thursday Jesus dropped to His knees in the position of a lowly slave to wash the feet of His disciples. The disciples were shocked and even embarrassed by this act of humility by the Lord of lords and King of kings. There is no instance in Jewish, Greco-Roman, or Mesopotamian sources of a superior washing the feet of an inferior.

Foot washing was dirty work, left for the poor and the lesser than. David and Kay, architects building homes for the rich and famous, were now building homes for the poor and needy. The thing about their work with Peggy is they not only made sure her feet were clean, but they also made sure she was bathed all over. Foot washing is an opportunity to learn what it means to be human—an understanding that we are all divine images of our Maker.

When Simon Peter refused to let Jesus wash his feet, He said, "What I am doing you do not understand now, but afterward you will understand" (John 13:7 ESV). Apparently, whatever meaning could be derived from foot washing was not immediately obvious to the disciples. Sure, washing was an example of being loving, but it also anticipated something. Something really, really important.

It wasn't just foot washing that was saved for the slaves. Crucifixion was a public way to deter any rebellion among the slave class. In 71 BC, after a slave rebellion was suppressed in Spartacus, more than six thousand slaves were crucified together along the Via Appia between Capua and Rome.[4] In other instances, if one slave was caught breaking the law, the entire slave community could be rounded up and crucified together, regardless of individual guilt.[5]

It is hardly an accident that crucifixion was so closely associated with the lowest possible class of the Roman caste system. The contrast of the two ideas—σταυρός [cross] and δοῦλος [slave]—were meant to serve as a compound to the social disgrace associated with both slavery and crucifixion in the ancient world. It was meant to remind people that there is, and always will be, an inferior and a superior. A greater than and a lesser than.

So we look toward Christ and His humble act of foot washing, and we see why the disciples were unable to immediately grasp the extreme significance of the act. Jesus lowered Himself to the position of a slave. He washed the disciples' feet as the lowest common denominator because He was ultimately preparing to die the dehumanizing death of a slave.

The connection is then made that cleaning out between the toes of the disciples' feet is akin to digging deep in our hearts and cleansing us from our sin. Everything about Christ's life demonstrated how the true kingdom's hierarchy is upside down, opposite of our world's social structure. Even to the degree that the King of kings rode in on a borrowed donkey.

He dropped to His knees to scrub away every ethnic and economic hierarchy from the church. As was His usual practice, He upset cultural norms. The fact that we still don't express an immense distrust of cultural norms to begin with surprises me.

But Jesus didn't stop there. He did them one better. He forced them to reevaluate everything they thought they knew.

My favorite painting is *The Incredulity of Saint Thomas* by Italian Baroque painter Caravaggio. Why? First off, like in all of his paintings, he has this way of combining a nitty-gritty reality with the hyperemotional through a dramatic use of lighting. Kind of like the Main Man he is depicting, he had a way of shaking tradition and ridding the idea of Greek-like gods by depicting Christ as thin and physically flawed.

Secondly, I am drawn to the expression on both Christ and Thomas's faces. There is an indescribable intimacy between the two, but Christ's expression also indicates a certain amount of displeasure or disappointment. Not because He is in pain but, rather, because He is weary of Thomas's need to feel the wound in order to believe. Understanding follows faith, not the converse.

Lastly, Christ insists through the painting that He is risen and alive, and He cares for us. So much so that we should not be abashed to thrust our own fingers into His side. In fact, He guides Thomas's finger into the wound as if to say that feeling the wound is just a different way of better understanding who He is. Against the realism of the painting, it insists on a faith based in reality—getting dirty and placing a finger in the wound.

Through His life and death, and even through artistic depictions thereafter (painted by an unbeliever no less), Christ calls us to get low in foot-washing-like service to one another. We are reminded that the Son of Man came to earth as a slave to serve us, to be crushed for (and by) us, to free us from our own slavery, and to open the way for us to enjoy and delight in

God's presence now and forever. We are called to stick our finger in the wound to experience His glory and fall to our own knees and weep because in that moment Thomas felt Christ's divinity and humanity. He realized that He had been suffering with us. He was fully man, journeying on earth with us, laughing, crying, and joking. He was reviled and affirmed, worshipped and beaten. He died and served.

———

I've seen many grown men turn into weeping piles of snot upon the realization they've been living life all wrong. They have failed to live a life worth living. Their own False Self has taken over, and they barely even know what it means to be truly human anymore.

But what is it to be human? What is it to suffer? Each person you pass on the street, in the grocery store, or at your place of work has had either a good or bad day. Each person you pass has a childhood. And every single person you pass on the street has something special about their story. Focus on that. Squint your one little eye and focus.

Aim.

Bull's-eye.

Peggy was truly special. She exuded it in miraculously beautiful handwriting and would use the brightest markers she could find to make artful note cards while she was tucked away safe in her little RV. Once she got the RV, it was pretty difficult to get her to leave it, and the only time she did willingly was to sell her note cards at a Christmas market. She said it was the first time she felt she could be her True Self and that the money she made that day was earned with dignity. This planted a seed in my brain that would mature and grow down the line.

The Christmas market was the last time we saw Peggy outside of her RV. We realized something was wrong when we'd call her and all we'd hear was her voice mail greeting. "Hi. It's Special P. Talk to me."

David would call.

Ring. Ring. Ring. Ring.

"Hi. It's Special P. Talk to me."

Kay would call.

Ring. Ring. Ring. Ring.

"Hi. It's Special P. Talk to me."

Tricia would call.

Ring. Ring. Ring. Ring.

"Hi. It's Special P. Talk to me."

Her voice mail message was a constant reminder of what was true but a frustrating thing nonetheless not to be able to reach her.

We knew that there was a girl staying with Peggy and that Peggy was excited for everyone to meet her. My inclination was that Peggy did not have too many friends. I knew, though, that having someone around could make it a lot easier for Peggy—making life a smidge more livable merely by having someone offer to reach the cereal on the top shelf. But we all had the feeling that something wasn't right. Tricia went over to Peggy's house, and the "friend" opened the door and said that Peggy was asleep. Tricia left and came back a few days later. Once again the friend said that Peggy was asleep. This time Tricia wouldn't take no for an answer. As Tricia made her way into Peggy's room, the girl started acting really nervous, becoming overly chatty and saying things about how Peggy had been having "such a difficult time falling asleep lately" so they should just let her sleep and not wake her.

When Tricia walked into the room, she got the willies. It was so quiet—quieter than your average quiet room. She went over to Peggy who was lying in bed, covers pulled up to her face and motionless. Her coloring looked terrible, so Tricia thought it was best to let her sleep and come back another day.

The following day Tricia got the call that Peggy had died.

The police and coroner called us, as the death had become a homicide investigation. Eventually they closed the case as a natural death. It was likely Peggy died and the friend didn't know what to do, so she left her there in her bed for hours, or days. Unfortunately, Peggy was notorious for being taken advantage of. Money would disappear regularly to pay for other people's drugs, other people's food, and other people's funerals. This was all a part of what made Special P so special. We knew that this girl was likely mooching off Peggy, and it was evident the way she started prowling around and claiming a landlord-tenant relationship.

Landlord-tenant relationship. Mother-daughter relationship. Peggy's life was filled with relationships that were anything but relational. While alone on the streets feeling less than human, her life changed once love entered it. I suppose I can't speak for Peggy about her relationship with David and Kay, but I can speak for David and Kay because they have told me time and time again what knowing Peggy has done for them.

Peggy gave David something that money can't buy.

The real treasure is the relationships you are building. David and Kay jumped into the abyss and started loving on other human beings. I think what we have to do is stop abdicating that responsibility to someone else and be willing to jump in, because the treasure trove of just jumping in is so enormous.

In the end David believed that he didn't help these people nearly as much as they helped him. One thing we all have in common is we can't take our stuff with us when we die, but we can hope to be reunited with the friendships formed on earth.

There's this story of a rich guy who got terminal cancer and was told he had only six months to live. He spent that night praying it up, saying, "God, I've been really blessed with what you've given me. I want to bring it with me."

God says, "Nah, man, you don't need all that stuff. It's nonsense."

But this guy just keeps pounding on the Lord and finally God relents, "Fine, bring it all with you. No problem. Bring all your treasure with you."

The guy is *pumped*. He's fantasizing, figuring out what he's going to bring and how he's going to get it there. Finally the guy dies and he ends up at the pearly gates. Peter's there, and the guy has his coffin full of all the stuff he wanted to bring.

Peter says, "Hey, man, welcome! But you don't need that here."

The guy says, "Well, I talked with the Lord, and He said I could bring my stuff with me."

Peter doesn't believe it. *The Lord wouldn't say that,* he

thinks. So he goes and checks and comes back, and shaking his head in disbelief says, "All right, He says you're good. That's incredible. So, what could you have possibly brought up here?"

The guy reaches over, opens the lid of the coffin, and it is lined with gleaming gold bars. It's absolutely beautiful.

And Peter looks at him and laughs. "Pavement?"

PHOTO BY MICHAEL O'BRIEN

CHAPTER 6

GORDY THE GENTLE GIANT

IT WAS LIKE SOMETHING OUT OF A FAIRY TALE, EXCEPT INSTEAD of a Renaissance-era king and queen, it was a badass Latino gangster and his wife.

Long ago (in 1979) in a faraway place near the mountains (Greeley, Colorado), on a cold winter's night, Linda Carmona was alone, asleep in her bed. Her husband, Tony, was still at the oil rig, knocking back his second, or third, or fourth beer.

They had recently moved to the dark and snowy hilltop, so Linda was surprised to hear a knock at the door. She had no idea who it could possibly be. When she opened the door, no one was there. She took a few steps to the edge of the porch, looked around, looked up, and then looked down to find a three-day-old baby naked in the snow. His soft and fragile rose-petal skin was against the packed mountain of ice. He lay there silently with the smallest gestures that hinted at desperation for touch, reaching his arms up at her, his eyes piercing Linda's heart. She swept him up and wrapped him in a blanket, holding him tightly against her chest. It was then she noticed the short note attached to his diaper.

I don't want him.
I never want to see him again.
Don't ever tell him who his mother is.

In that moment Linda knew that this was the newborn son of her crack-addict half sister, and in that same moment Linda thanked God for this gift of a child. She began shaking and cooing and pacing the floor waiting for Tony to get home from the oil field so he could go back out to get diapers and formula.

At the stroke of midnight, Tony arrived.

If you were sitting on the couch when Tony walked in the door, your back might've straightened, your muscles might've tightened, and your eyes might've widened. You would've been able to tell that this guy does not mess around. A blue bandanna around his head framed three inked teardrops falling from his left eye. When he took off his coat, you could see the etches of one-dimensional prison tattoos—a cobweb, a five-point crown, hearts with ribbon banners, ornate crosses, skulls, thorns, and, unexpectedly, a unicorn and a cockatiel. His face was weathered and his eyes were like slits. Nowadays, he's only got one good leg, so I can only imagine this aggressive limp demanding more authority. He tongued the lower gums in his mouth slowly and methodically, like some kind of commanding gesture as he scanned the room.

"Tony!" Linda didn't explain anything other than exclaiming, "You need to go to the store and get me some formula and diapers for the baby!"

"You crazy, Linda? Baby?"

She pointed to the bedroom, where she had bundled the baby and put him in a cardboard box lined with blankets.

Tony's lead foot slowly made its way to the room where, sure enough, there was this unaccounted for baby.

Now, a man with a short temper might be expected to explode, and this was something Tony was particularly notorious for. So, really, it was anyone's guess, including Linda's, what might happen. But no one could have guessed that Tony would reach down to the bundled baby, bring the small, still-cold, smooth skin to his leathery face to kiss it on the cheek and shed real-life saltwater tears.

"How, Linda?"

She handed him the note, and it quickly registered with him too. Linda's half sister had abandoned this baby. When they eventually got a hold of her, they made the deal that they would hand over all food stamps and SSI (Supplemental Security Income) checks in order to keep the baby. They both knew that the baby boy's biological mother didn't care about her child as much as using those checks to buy more cocaine so she could pepper the world with more abandoned children—which she did. So with the money from the oil field alone, Tony fed his wife and child.

They named him Gordy. It wasn't (and likely isn't) to their knowledge, but the name Gordon is Scottish and means "spacious fort."[1] Turns out they were spot-on because by age five he looked like he could be ten, weighing more than seventy pounds. He was a spacious fort for sure.

It was at this age, five years old, that Gordy had his first seizure.

They took him to the hospital, and the doctors asked Linda if she had done any drugs while she was pregnant with Gordy. She gave them the full story, including her sister's addiction and how he had been left in the snow. They left the hospital with an epilepsy diagnosis and a verdict that his brain would likely never develop beyond the capability of a seven-year-old. At home, life shakily returned to a new normal, interrupted by Gordy's regular convulsions and hospitalizations. Money was tight and medical bills stacked up, but the Carmonas had hope and they had each other.

When Gordy went to school, he had a hard time with the other kids. He didn't know how to say "Excuse me." If a kid had a leg sticking out he would just keep walking, taking that leg with him. Zero social skills.

It was not easy raising Gordy, especially while Linda was a single mother during Tony's stay in an Oklahoma prison for stolen property. So while he was locked up and unable to be contacted, Linda and Gordy headed to Austin, Texas, for a much-needed fresh start. However, they still hoped they would eventually hear from Tony and they could all reunite. The three of them loved each other. They only had each other. Tony grew up in a gang community, so he was taught by his entire family to do what he needed to survive, even if that meant stealing. Tony, being the oldest, was given the task of teaching his brothers and sisters to do the same. He eventually left to avoid the bad effects his family had on him, and the bad effects he had on his family—a hard thing to do for a gang member. That's how Linda and Gordy became his everything.

When Tony finally got out of the clink, he heard that Linda and his now twenty-year-old Gordy were in Austin. He hopped a southbound Greyhound and was dropped off right by Sixth Street and I-35, under the overpass where he spotted a guy with long hair and a dog. You see, Tony loves dogs. To this day he dreams of escaping to a home in the desert with hundreds of them. So upon seeing the dog, he made his way to the fuzzy friend only to discover that this man was part of a crowd under the bridge listening to a church sermon. Tony thought, *Hell, I don't have anything else to do,* so he stood there in the back and listened. The guy who was preaching started praying for people, and he rested his hand on the back of a tall young man. Tony thought, *Man, that kid looks just like my Gordy.* He pushed his way to the front, moving up little by little. Linda was short, so he couldn't see her, but he kept his eyes fixed on the guy who appeared to be his son. It was only once he'd made his way to the very front that he confirmed it really was Gordy and that it was Linda right next to him. She was also being prayed for. When Gordy saw Tony he took off, bounding and lunging to embrace him.

The preacher, Brother Dwayne, asked, "Who are you?"

"This boy's father," Tony replied.

This reunion, though sweet, began a three-year stretch on the streets of spending nights in a cardboard box or separated from each other at the shelter. Many of the shelters wouldn't take the Carmonas due to Gordy's epilepsy. The ones that did take them often put the family in the hallway that separated the men from the women, just so Gordy's seizures didn't wake the others at the shelter.

A number of reasons made having Gordy around difficult. He was a boy trapped in a large man's body, taking up way more than half of the space that the three of them would share. He had male urges but a seven-year-old's innocence. He was another mouth to feed and another thirst to quench. But

Gordy was consistently considered a blessing—his humor and joyfulness bringing a light to the family.

Gordy also had a way of noticing things missed by others, and he exuded a constant sense of hope. Once, the three of them were walking down South Congress looking for some spare change, and Gordy was lagging behind. He suddenly ran up to them, saying, "I'm hungry! Let's go get some lunch!" Devastated to tell their son for the 432nd time that they had no money for lunch, Gordy then waved a twenty-dollar bill in the air. "Yes, we do!" Linda and Tony had no idea where he found it. The two of them were feet in front of him, scouring the pavement. Linda insisted that it was magic, and that day they were able to fill their bellies with cheeseburgers, french fries, and chocolate malts.

Later that week in the enchanted forest where their single tent dwelled, the Carmonas got fleas. I met the Carmonas right around this time—in 2005—covered in sores from the flea-bites. For years the three of them continued to go to the church under the bridge and the regular Tuesday night Bible study. At one of those Bible studies, Brother Dwayne introduced us, and it just so happened earlier that same week I was forced to repossess an RV from one of our other friends in another chapter—the "spicy" man. He had trashed the place with crack pipes in the curtain rods, porno on the floor, and condoms strewn everywhere. It took seven full days for the five of us to clear out the RV, so we put the Carmonas in the Bel-Air Hotel until it was available. This was a weekly hotel dedicated to those living at the lowest economic level.

Seven days later, they walked into the 2006 Jay Flight RV filled with food, drinks, pots, and pans. They moved around the room touching everything, gasping at the sofa and the kitchen table, and opening the shower door and *oohing* and *ahhing*. They ran their fingers down the fabric curtains. Gordy's big, toothy mouth was at a loss for words—the first and last time I ever witnessed that. He threw himself onto the sofa, arms stretched out, and closed his eyes as Tony hugged Linda. We left the family to enjoy their new home.

When Gordy woke up the next morning, Tony and Linda were still asleep. He bounced onto their bed, yelling, "Dad! Mom! Get up! Dad, it's time. We got to check out or they're going to throw us out!" His mind couldn't register that they had a place to live.

And like some divine reversal of all the times Tony had to tell Gordy *there isn't enough*, or *I know it's cold, but you've got to go to sleep*, or *I know you're thirsty but we don't have any water*, he was finally able to tell his son, "You don't got to worry. You're home."

It took him more than two months to realize they were going to have a place to stay long-term.

The Carmonas almost immediately became a part of the Mobile Loaves family. Linda began working at the commissary, and Tony volunteered every single day, taking three different buses across town to get there. Gordy always offered to serve lemonade when it needed to be served. The family, still in unbelievable poverty, donated twenty-five dollars a month to the organization.

We have a fund-raising philosophy at MLF called the HP ratio, where H is the numerator and P is the denominator. H stands for heart and P for pocket. The bigger the heart the bigger the whole number is. The Carmonas had a ginormous HP ratio, given the amount of money that they earned and how much they gave.

Gordy loved riding around in the food trucks. He would hear the rumble of the pickup coming toward his RV and come leaping out of the front door. It was his dream to drive one someday, but he would never even be allowed a license because of his epilepsy. He told everyone that one day he wanted to work for Mobile Loaves. So I asked him, "Gordy, what do you want to do?"

"Mr. Alan," he said, "I want to do what you do."

"Well, what is it that you think I do?"

"Well, I can stand up and point. I can do that." He scrunched up his face and put one hand on his hip and started pointing around—left then right then left again. "See?"

Yeah, pretty much all I do.

Gordy also had a lifelong dream of being a Boy Scout. But, as most of us know, you can't be a Boy Scout after the age of eighteen. So at age twenty-six, we found a troop willing to take him in and a uniform big enough to fit this big, hulking, more-than-two-hundred-pound man-kid. I've never in my life seen such pride. On a day that he was able to wear his Boy Scout uniform and ride in the trucks, he looked like his face would explode with pure elation.

But that excitement was just a taste of what was to come at the Tap Out Ceremony—an evening that proved this fairy tale was indeed magical.

That night, Gordy sat cross-legged, towering alongside the several hundred other Boy Scouts. He gazed at the staff costumed in Native American clothing, sitting in a circle around the fire. He shook nervously, his palms holding his ankles, his back straight, and his eyes bright. The older Boy Scouts (but not older than Gordy) danced around, tapping several kids on the shoulders to be nominated to be a part of the more formal Order of the Arrow ceremony. The air was electric for Gordy, so we didn't have the heart to tell him that because of his age he was disqualified from being chosen (just like we didn't have the heart to tell him that Selena Gomez was actually not his girlfriend). But he was only about seven years old developmentally, so how do you tell a seven-year-old they are too old for Boy Scouts?

Well, something miraculous happened that night and Gordy got tapped. Maybe this is some weird Peter Pan or Pinocchio scenario and Gordy became the age that he was in his mind. Maybe the kid that was tapping out the scouts had his hand too low, and it just happened to brush Gordy's soaring head. But the moment that scout touched Gordy, he popped out of his seat into the air like a beanstalk. It ended up being the best night of Gordy's life, which, though we didn't know it at the time, was going to be a short one.

———∿∿∿———

Summer turned to fall and fall turned to winter, and on December 8, Linda received word that her mother had died. So she headed to Denver, Colorado, to be with her family. Though still married, Tony remained in the RV and Linda lived in a nearby apartment with Gordy. She was hesitant to leave Gordy alone due to his condition. When she left she told him, "Don't leave this house. I'll be back in a couple of days. *Te amo*, my Big Bear."

"What about if I want pizza?"

"You can have it delivered."

At 1:00 a.m. the phone rang at Linda's friend's house in Colorado. Her friend picked up and then handed it to Linda. "I think something is wrong. It's Gordy. Why would he call so late?"

Linda clutched the phone to her ear. "Gordy? What is it? Are you okay?"

"I lied to you, Mama. I walked to the pizza place. I'm so sorry, Mama. I love you."

"I miss you, Gordy."

"Oh! I miss you so much too! When are you coming home?"

"It'll only be a couple of days."

"I love you, Mama!"

"Love you, Big Bear."

The next evening at sundown, Pat Patterson, one of the Six-Pack and one of the founders of Mobile Loaves, went to check on Gordy at the apartment. He knocked on the front door, but no one answered. He banged and still nothing. Knowing Gordy was supposed to be there, Pat hurried to the side of the building and found the window into Linda's bedroom was cracked just a little bit. He slid the window up and climbed through to hear the sound of rushing water. When he got to the hallway, he took a step on the carpeted floors, feeling water pool around his feet. He looked down the hallway and saw water pouring from the opening at the bottom of the bathroom door. Hesitating for only a moment, Pat pushed the door open against the pressure of the water on the door.

There was Gordy, lying naked and quiet, the same way he appeared to the Carmonas thirty-three years earlier. He drowned from a seizure in the bathtub.

Pat called Tony and he arrived just as the sun was setting and the cops, investigators, and coroners were arriving.

By the time Tricia and I got to the apartment, it was dark, and Pat and Tony were standing in the parking lot among a crowd of officials and behind the yellow tape—a blockade keeping Tony a hundred feet from his son. It felt like a hundred miles. It's funny how on vivid and noisy nights like that one, everything seems calm and quiet. Everything seems slightly to the left of reality. Pat, Tony, and I pleaded with the investigators to see Gordy, but, for some reason still unknown to me, they wouldn't allow it.

I remember looking at Tony as all this was happening.

You look at him and see a rough and raging Mexican gang member with tattoo teardrops under his eyes. If you're a bystander removed from the situation—removed from a friendship with Tony—you'd think something else was going on. His tough and craggy skin reflected the flashing red and blue lights from the cop cars, exposing a face of pure rage. You'd think, *What did that guy just do, and why isn't he in handcuffs?* If you never became friends with this guy, you'd never get to discover what an awesome human being he is. And you wouldn't get to hear the fairy tale of Gordy the Gentle Giant.

We judge people based on external appearances and actions. *Tony? Oh, he's bad. He stole a bunch of crap and did some drugs and went to prison for two years! Linda? Why would she marry a guy like Tony? And their son? Probably a crack baby who doesn't get the support he needs from two neglecting parents.*

God judges *moral* choices. Based on what we know for sure, if we were to judge Tony on moral choices, we'd see a man raised in a gang who took a baby in from off the streets when he barely had enough to survive himself. When we see a man who has been raised with the understanding that cruelty is the *right* thing, and then that man rescues an abandoned, mentally challenged baby and loves him to the ends of the earth and back, he just may be doing more impressive work than someone else, raised respectably and securely, by giving up his life for a friend. C. S. Lewis put it this way:

> Some of us who seem like quite nice people may, in fact, have made so little use of a good heredity and good upbringing that we are really worse than those whom we regard as friends. . . . That is why Christians are told not to judge. We see only the results which a man's choices make out of his raw material. But God does not judge him on the raw material at all, but on what he has done with it.
>
> Most of the man's psychological makeup is probably due to his body: when his body dies all that will fall off him, and the real central man, the thing that chose, that made the best or worst out of this material, will stand naked. All sorts of nice things which we thought our own, but which were really due to a good digestion, will fall off some of us: all sorts of nasty things which were due to complexes or bad health will fall off others. We shall then, for the first time, see every one as he really was. There will be surprises.[2]

What a surprise, indeed.

I always say the secret to my "success" is *keep it simple, stupid.* Christ, knowing that we are stupid, and knowing that we need things broken down nice and easy for us, gave a blunt

and absolute command in just three words: "Do not judg_
(Matthew 7:1).

Pretty simple. But again, we had to go and complicate
it. Seldom do we step outside of ourselves to really grasp the
needs and feelings of another person. If only we could make
more of an effort to experience the feelings of another person,
the world would be much more compassionate, and our tapes-
tries—be it your personal tapestry or the tapestry of the entire
human experience—would be far more vivid.

Because how can we judge what we don't understand?

Besides, if the journey to becoming fully human is to discover who you are, the first step to answering that question is
realizing that you are a member of the huge human family—that
we are all brothers and sisters, whatever your background and
whatever your past. Remember that life doesn't need to be perfect to look like a fairy tale. The minute you can accept that, the
closer you are to knowing the secret of what it is to be human.

Becoming fully human is really the acceptance and
realization that no human is more *human* than any other
human—which, surprisingly, is the core of most of today's
problems. Think about this in light of many current issues.
Abortion? One human life considered more important than
another human life. Terrorism? One human life considered
more important than another human life. Racism? One human
life considered more important than another human life.

How can anyone justify being more human than someone else?

Guess what? They can't.

It comes down to the need for a universal respect for
human life.

Gordy, when viewed under the microscope that most people use to judge the value of a human being, would be considered more of an inconvenience than anything.

Our feeling of being inconvenienced has bred a culture of death. If we are willing to go inside that womb and kill a baby, and then on the other hand take our aging parents into the most disgusting, noisy, desperate, and lonely spaces, why not just line up our homeless people and shoot them? Just roll up a truck, flip up the flap, and start mowing them down to fall into the ditch. That's the culture we have created. That's the moral decline of America, and the disrespect for human life is almost a distinctly Western problem. Tony and Linda taught me that no human being could ever be an inconvenience. Their story of taking this baby, raising him, and loving him taught me a lesson in a very real and tangible way—but that would come later.

We stood around for about three hours until Gordy was brought out, covered in a blanket on a gurney. This is when Tony lost it—emotion poured out of him like a water faucet turned all the way to the right. He lunged toward the cops and I attempted to hold him back. After all that waiting around, wondering exactly what they could be spending that much time doing, the coroners wheeled the gurney into the car in about three seconds.

I don't know how I got tapped to go with Linda and Tony to get Gordy's ashes, but there we were, the three of us riding along and thinking how happy Gordy would be to be riding in the truck. I'm in the driver's seat and Tony is in the passenger seat holding the wooden box filled with Gordy, and it's heavier than any urn I can remember.

Tony asked, "Mr. Alan, will you let Gordy drive?" as he moved the box across the console and into my lap. This motion released a blend of emotion—guttural heaving in reaction to Gordy's death and the humor of Gordy now being in the driver's seat. You only get to witness the confluence of those emotions when you elect to dive into the grittiness of building relationships with other broken and battered human beings. The fruit of those relationships is enormous.

I took the urn and placed him between my right knee and the steering wheel. The size of the urn felt like an appropriate size for Gordy—small, like what he always should have been. At the stoplight I closed my eyes and imagined Gordy's seven-year-old spirit. I thought back to the last Christmas when I was dressed like Santa Claus and he sat on my lap, a full-grown adult, beaming and wearing the toothiest of grins.

And there he was, a box of fairy dust, with his wish finally granted—driving the truck like he always dreamed he would.

I believe that among all the fairy tales that have ever been told, dating back hundreds and hundreds of centuries, Gordy is one of the few who truly lived happily ever after.

PHOTO BY MICHAEL O'BRIEN

CHAPTER 7

LAURA TANIER WAS AN ENGINEER

LAURA TANIER ALWAYS KNEW SHE WAS DIFFERENT.

She was born and raised in the Four Corners region of New Mexico on a Navajo reservation in Shiprock. She lived in a crowded hogan—a round house made of mud and wood—and found few friendships in the other members of her tribe.

Her father was an Englishman, her mother was Navajo, and just like her heritage crossed boundaries, so did everything else about her. Laura was born an incredibly intelligent, kind, and creative boy.

As she grew older, it dawned on her that the reservation could never provide the opportunities she desired, so Laura took a bus to Austin, Texas, at the age of twelve in the hopes of mastering technology and returning to her tribe to teach them all she would learn. Despite staggering personal struggles Laura persevered and received her GED, a bachelor's degree, and a master's degree in electrical engineering from the University of Texas, all while living on the streets with nothing but a few changes of clothes and a bulky laptop computer.

She was an unusual hero who walked the streets of Austin

slowly and methodically with a crooked ever-ready smile, blond-gray curls that bobbed out of control, a layered outfit depending on the weather—but always including a dress or skirt and oftentimes a bucket hat, a plastic bag that held her precious belongings, and a five o'clock shadow that she never managed to take care of despite all of the other changes she had made. She was likable enough to have the gender reassignment surgery performed by a random doctor who heard her story and decided to do the work pro bono.

I met Laura in Wooldridge Park on the first Street Retreat, the same night we met J. P. Laura is another reason that weekend remains the best of my life.

—※—

Judy Knotts is a sixty-two-year-old PhD, Catholic school principal, and fellow Street Retreater who had spent the night in the safe house, behind the protection of a gate, and had decided to hang out with us bad boys the next day. As dusk started setting in, Judy asked me if she could sleep alongside the homeless—actually on the streets instead of in the safe house or in the protected alleyway.

Laura had overheard Judy's request and said, "You come stay with me; those men use bad language."

This, as you can imagine, was the least of Judy's concerns, yet she still decided to stay with Laura at her camp. It was an abandoned small office building downtown where she slept on a second-floor porch. She offered Judy the first-floor porch and gave her two presents—a new piece of cardboard to sleep on and an empty peanut butter jar to pee in. Judy used the cardboard, but not the jar. After talking for a few hours, the two hit the hay around midnight, and Laura woke Judy up around five in the morning to avoid the police sweeps.

Laura then took Judy to the First United Methodist Church to get in line early for free breakfast. The two spent the next few days together wandering the streets, looking for free food, going to Mass (Laura was not Catholic), and praying. In an incredible leap of faith and friendship, Laura gave Judy the only copy of a book she was writing. On the final night of the retreat, Judy found a flashlight and read the entire handwritten manuscript that was nearly three inches thick. It was her autobiography that told the tale of a young boy not feeling comfortable in his skin, of unloving parents, of leaving the land of inopportunity and fighting for an education in a big city. Laura wrote about transformation, of finding convention difficult to swallow—not because she didn't want to, but because she frankly didn't know how—all the while weaving art, science, religion, history, music, and fantasy into her own personal narrative. Some of her writing was so intricate that even Judy with her PhD could barely keep up and follow what she was saying. One thing that stood out to Judy was that she didn't write much about anyone else because she didn't have anyone else to write about.

As you can imagine Laura didn't know a lot of people like her—a transgender, homeless genius who grew up on a technologically underdeveloped Native American reservation and on her own by age twelve. She broke every stereotype that could possibly be attributed to her. She never touched drugs and alcohol and spent her time volunteering at homeless shelters when she wasn't writing, painting, or studying.

Of all the people I've ever known, Laura is one of the most Christlike. She was a tormented teacher of compassion and tolerance in a way that is difficult to wrap your mind around.

Think of it this way: Laura and I are two *very* different-looking threads—the moment we cross paths and interconnect, not only does the whole tapestry become stronger, the whole thing becomes way more vivid and beautiful. We should all know by now that diversity makes for a rich tapestry, and we must understand that all the threads in the tapestry are equal in value. But the tapestry cannot be strong unless these threads are firmly intertwined. However, if we treated our threads the way we treat most of our relationships, the whole thing would fall apart.

This is why Laura taught me a unity *beyond* diversity.

Most often, we know people on a conceptual level—name, their hobbies, where they work. Instead, what we should know of ourselves and others is what makes the muscles in our fingers tingle, what makes our hearts beat or our blood rush. This is a universal truth I've discovered about my homeless brothers and sisters: because they have nothing to hide and nothing to lose, we're able to skip superficial small talk. We can skip job titles or what they "do," their favorite local restaurants, how they like the way their car drives, etc. We can jump right into the nitty-gritty real talk because two things are going on here:

1. The conversation isn't rooted in trying to get at a person's similarities and differences on a superficial level (which is what most conversations try to get at), so the new relationship is able to skip the typical strained conversation. Often we project our own

thoughts and beliefs upon strangers and make judgments based on how we think they should be living their lives (i.e., a Volvo is better than a Volkswagen).

2. The conversation surpasses even thinking about diversity because the focus becomes less about *Wow, look how we're different* and moves into *Wow, look how much we're the same.* It reaches a profound place of exploring the very basic truths of what makes us human—the necessities of life when it comes to food and water, but also love and kindness—and that's a very unifying place (i.e., we all have this desire to see the world—a Volvo or a Volkswagen is just the means to an end).

What you can know of the world is similar to putting a finger in a glass of water. With that finger you can explore the parameters of the glass. You can feel the edges. You can feel how deep the water is.

This is how you interact with what is possible to know.

To comprehend the unknown, you should think about putting your finger in the ocean. This unity-beyond-diversity deal taught me the beauty of being taken out of the self. Of moving from a glass of water into an ocean—because aren't we all drawn to the ocean for some mysterious reason?

We must appreciate the richness of difference, while realizing that our own differences are the very thing that unifies us under our Creator.

But the majority of us can't grasp that. We stay trapped behind our social media description facades and our hip clothes so we can project the image we want to project. We rarely get into raw and real conversations; we don't let the world open up, or even ourselves, so it creates another universal problem that every person experiences. It's like a riddle:

What is the one thing everybody experiences but no one can really talk about? What is the one thing every one of us has in common and is the very thing that keeps us isolated?

Loneliness.

Laura existed in a vacuum.

Seven hundred years ago, Mechthild of Magdeburg, a Benedictine nun and poet, had a vision of a lonely God in a vacuum who, out of such loneliness, created humanity and entered into a loving relationship with it. She saw a God who wanted to create humanity in order to complete Himself through a relationship with His creation and, in doing so, break His own splendid isolation. Sure, this is a very unorthodox vision, but it still kinda sorta reveals something about our God, who eventually became a man Himself.

God is lonely for us as much as we are lonely for Him. He is the one who has always been foolishly in love with us. And even though God is complete in Himself, He acts as if He is incomplete without us. As Mechthild said, "God has enough of everything, caressing human souls is the only thing he cannot get enough of."[1]

At the very core of our human spirit, we have a need to love with great passion and a need to be loved unconditionally. Our happiness is contingent on loving and being loved, so we go on longing and searching for the source of this happiness—the object of love that will satisfy this need.

As Saint Augustine put it, our hearts are *inquietum,* or "restless." In the first paragraph of *The Confessions of Saint Augustine,* Augustine penned his now-famous line, "You stir man to take pleasure in praising you, because you have made us for yourself, and our heart is restless until it finds its rest in you."[2] There seems to be an inconsolable restlessness that refuses to be soothed by anything or anyone other than God Himself. This deep restless desire reminds us of a vast separation between God and us.

This restlessness stems from not exactly knowing what we are looking for—so we look for it in salaries, cars, makeup, clothes, crack cocaine, alcohol—but it is an aching for a certain something. It feels like the hopeless longing for a home we've felt but never been to.

Another word that speaks to this concept is the German word *Sehnsucht.* It is one of those words that doesn't quite have an English equivalent, but it is often translated as "longing." This word took on a particular significance for C. S. Lewis, as he described it as the inconsolable longing that is always waiting for fulfillment in an unknowable something, somewhere.[3] In his pilgrimage into Christianity, Lewis met his friend Owen Barfield, who quickened this longing in an "idea of the spiritual world as home—the discovery of homeliness in that is otherwise so remote—the feeling that you are coming back tho' to a place you have never yet reached."[4] In the afterword to the third edition of *The Pilgrim's Regress,* he provided examples of what sparked this desire in him particularly.

That unnameable something, desire for which pierces us
like a rapier at the smell of bonfire, the sound of wild ducks

flying overhead, the title of *The Well At the World's End*, the opening lines of "Kubla Khan", the morning cobwebs in late summer, or the noise of falling waves.[5]

A home we've felt but never been to—a place of intended permanence, a dwelling place, a storied place, a safe resting place. The place from which we were displaced.

So when God became incarnate, so did loneliness.

Jesus is incredibly acquainted with the devastating effect of loneliness. "He was despised and rejected by men, a man of sorrows and acquainted with grief" (Isaiah 53:3 ESV).

Imagine, if you will, what living in this world was like for Jesus. He was without sin. Imagine what His childhood was like. He would have stuck out like a moral sore thumb, never quite fitting in. No one likes the "teacher's pet" in class—always on assignment, telling the truth, signing up for extracurricular activities, and seemingly a big know-it-all. Now multiply that, and you've got a piece of how annoying Jesus probably seemed to His classmates.

Even His loving parents, knowing His true being, wouldn't have fully understood Him. Nor would they have been able to protect Him from the stinging remarks of others.

Jesus was a sinless person living with sinful parents, sinful brothers and sisters, sinful friends, and sinful neighbors. Quite literally, no one on earth could identify with Him. No human being could put an arm around Him as He sat in tears and say, "I know exactly what you're going through."

I mean, He was the Son of God for God's sake.

Fast-forward through a life of loneliness.

Now, can you imagine what it would be like to be hanging

on the cross, exhausted beyond comprehension because the people you love just beat you to a pulp, and being the only person ever to experience what you are experiencing? (Also imagine, in that moment, being the only person in the world to truly know what love means.)

No one has ever experienced what it is like to be the Son of God, and not even God (up until Christ's incarnation) had experienced what it was like to be man. That's got to be the epitome of loneliness. Ever been in a conversation and you said something like, "Yeah, I got fired today. I don't know what I am going to do. I feel like I'm drowning, you know what I mean?" and everyone in that group kind of side-eyes each other, their bottom lips slip to the side, and their heads dance back and forth kind of like, "Eh, actually we don't," and you want to melt away and cry a thousand tears? Well, someone somewhere has been fired before. Someone somewhere could relate to you in that moment. Now imagine that no one in the history of human existence has experienced the sting of being sacked. That is, in an incredibly and dangerously oversimplified microcosmic sense, what it would feel like to be Jesus.

However, Jesus' loneliness reached its apex the moment He became sin for us on the cross and was "forsaken" by His Father. He grew up estranged by sinlessness, and then by taking on every sin known to man. He was there experiencing what no one had experienced before or since, enduring at that one little tiny point in space and time all that sin deserved.

Most of the time we focus on the physical suffering of the crucifixion—the whipping, the crown of thorns, and His immolation on the cross. But the real suffering comes after the beatings, after the taunting of the crowd, after the darkness had covered the land—it came in a moment of long silence, embodied in an anguished cry from the depths of the Savior's soul:

"My God, my God, why have you forsaken me?" (Matthew 27:46)

Ultimate isolation.

This is the culmination of the passion of the Christ.

Passion comes from the Latin *pati*, which means "to suffer." So compassion comes from the Latin *com-* + *pati*—"to suffer with." This is God wanting to experience human loneliness, the greatest suffering that a human can experience. The compassion of Christ.

Ask any homeless person what the most difficult part of being homeless is.

It's not hunger.

It's not sleep deprivation.

It's not bug bites or infection.

The single most difficult part of being homeless is loneliness. No one knowing your name. The way people look at you. Dying on the street and both your life and death going wholly unnoticed.

The *Merriam-Webster* definition of *compassion* is "sympathetic consciousness of others' distress together with a desire to alleviate it."[6] That's exactly why Laura wins the award for most Christlike. She understood what it was to be compassionate in an almost inhuman sense—way beyond my peon brain at least. She happily suffered with others in order to, in some way, alleviate the suffering.

For some reason there is this one particular memory of

Laura that stands out to me. I was on a truck run with about twenty young middle-school kids, ages twelve to thirteen years old. We had a bunch of huge cans of Wolf Brand Chili and super-sized bags of Fritos, and were serving Frito pie (for all non-Texans, this is the most delicious quick meal known to man). All the kids were lined up on one side of the truck filling up the red-and-white-checkered paper concession boats with Fritos. The back of the truck has two doors—one that opens up and one that pulls down like a table. So I was standing at the end of the truck scooping on a heaping load of chili—using the table to set the bowls of Frito pie on. Well, this one kid came up to me and exclaimed, "Mr. Graham! Mr. Graham! We're almost out of Fritos!"

Good news: we had some more bags of Fritos on the other side of the truck. Bad news: as I was heading to the side of the truck, the corner of the metal table hit me right in the gonads, and I was down for the count, keeling over in writhing pain.

Suddenly, I felt these giant hands on my shoulders and a deep, feminine, and gentle voice asking, "Alan, are you all right?" I looked up between my squinted eyelids, and as the whole world spun around, I saw Laura standing there, her long and big arms coming around me and lifting me up off of the parking lot ground.

There was something so extraordinarily gentle about Laura.

Because she couldn't give money, she devoted her life to giving back. She helped organize and distribute donated clothing to women, she tutored in math and science, she worked at the local food pantry, and her charity was so beyond average because of the amount of love she gave it that she was recognized and received an award for her volunteer work.

One day, Laura was sexually assaulted. When she got on the bus to go home, she suffered a stroke. The combination of the assault and stroke led to severe depression, which eventually caused her to lose her engineering job and her house. But despite the assault, the stroke, the job loss, and the eviction, she was never—not for one moment—bitter. She viewed every negative event of her life as circumstantial, never asked for a handout, and never blamed anyone for anything.

She did not point a finger, even on the day a car ran a red light at a busy intersection, hitting her and sending her to the emergency room.

Judy, who was used to hearing from Laura on a weekly basis, got nervous when she couldn't get ahold of her. So she called around asking to see if anybody knew where Laura was. Finally, she got word that Laura was at Brackenridge Hospital. Judy hurried over to the hospital to see if Laura was okay, and was relieved to find her not in critical condition, but frustrated that the doctors would not allow her to visit. So she wrote Laura a note and left, eager to see her when she was released. A few days later, however, the injuries starting showing signs of a staph infection and suddenly, without notice or warning, Laura died totally alone in the hospital.

Just as Christ had died alone, Laura died alone.

If you haven't picked this up already, Christ was homeless on earth. He was a homeless man. Like Matthew 8:20 says: "Foxes have holes and the birds of the air have nests, but the Son of Man has nowhere to lay His head" (NASB). This particular loneliness that God the Son experienced parallels many of our homeless brothers and sisters, but none more so than Laura Tanier—a heartbreakingly beautiful blend of ongoing compassion and total isolation. It wasn't until Christ experienced the climax of loneliness while dying completely alone on the cross that He was able to finally, after His thirty-three years on earth, reunite with and annihilate loneliness alongside His Father.

———

I like to imagine heaven being the best cocktail party ever—no small talk, only heart-to-hearts, with a constant and ever-flowing undercurrent of joy. Like God's love, this party is filled with abundance. The very best booze is being served; the finest, most renowned mixologists in all the world are pouring these strong drinks in glasses with long stems. Beautiful music is filling the air. And the most important factor of any successful party—the conversation. Yes, the conversation is profoundly unadulterated and sincerity-filled. People aren't walking on eggshells; the truth is exposed and love conquers all.

God makes Gatsby look like an amateur.

And here's the deal: I truly believe that at this incredible cocktail party, Christ will be particularly eager to have long conversations with people like Laura Tanier, because Laura Tanier was aware of what it means to treat people with compassion and love on earth. Sure, I can't understand everything about Laura, but that isn't for me to understand. It is more important that I listen and learn from how she was able to consistently embody God's love for everyone.

Christ is going to want to talk to those people because they loved people without judgments and boundaries despite being chastised for it. In this strange way, Laura's extreme uniqueness allowed her to find a way to relate to everybody, and, yet, no one could relate to her. She, like Jesus, forever existed on the fringe—spit upon, assaulted, and persecuted.

The irony (and we all know God's got a clever sense of humor) is that if we could have the conversation that we are going to have at the big cocktail party in the sky, I think we would be able to get rid of all the problems we've got going on down here. We'd be able to completely rid the world of loneliness and misunderstanding because we wouldn't be afraid to love and be loved. Remember that before Christ experienced the most extreme isolation, He also gave us ultimate communion in Him at a dinner table. It's that communion that could alleviate all the world's suffering.

The reason God created us is rooted in relationship. The reason we exist on this world shoulder to shoulder with millions of other human beings is relationship. And yet we still give our brothers and sisters what *we* think they need. It's not a job. It's not a house. It's not a car. It's the abundant love of Jesus Christ. That love is so abundant that it flows through you and calls you to be abundant too—to help provide the things like jobs and houses that they need to survive. It becomes like planning the best cocktail party ever. *I want to throw the best cocktail party ever known for the people I love, and I want to make sure it has everything it needs for everyone to have the most wonderful time.* And so the checklist begins: *Food?* Check. *Drink?* Check. *Guest list?* Check.

And guess what? We're all invited!

We live in a society that discounts the value and insight of people like Laura and Danny when, in reality, they're the ones who understand what all of us really need—and, more often than not, they've given it to me tenfold.

I think it's time now that you and I change the way people view how we are to serve people—that it's not with an attitude that says, "Here's your need. Here's your meal unit. Here's your cot. Here's your bread and your juice." But rather, it starts with you and I participating—not with our checkbooks, but with our lives. Allowing our threads to be so intertwined that their suffering is *our* suffering.

It's with our relationships and our willingness to befriend another human being.

It's with love.

Remember that Communion without sacrificial love is just bread and wine. Don't just give the homeless a handout—give them your hand.

PHOTO BY MICHAEL O'BRIEN

CHAPTER 8

THE LOVE STORY OF
BRÜK AND ROBIN

IF EVER THERE WAS A BAD BOY, IT WAS BRÜK KEENER—A CHAR-
ismatic guy with a pretty face and smart as a whip. He could
walk out of a bar without ever paying for a drink and would
usually leave with two bottles of champagne in his denim
jacket for the road (either coming from the lovestruck bartender or his own sticky fingers).

It was 2004 and Brük was sitting in a bar that was mostly
empty—except for a girl who sat about five stools down from
him talking to a friend. This girl noticed him and asked her
friend, "Who is that guy? I've never seen him in here before."

"You don't know Brük? Robin, you would be great together!
Go over there and talk to him!" Brük was a well-acquainted
guy in the neighborhood, both for his memorable swagger and
his status as a popular dope dealer.

Robin had just broken up with her boyfriend and wasn't
too interested in talking to any guys anytime soon, but, suddenly, she found her feet taking her over to Brük, grabbing the
stool right next to him, and offering to buy him a drink.

"Sure. I'm drinking rum and Coke."

"If you're going to drink with me, you'll drink what I get you, and it'll be a beer. Hey, bartender, two Busches!"

The two liked each other right away and decided to go ride their bikes to see what trouble they could get themselves into. But before they could get anywhere, Brük was already saying the wrong things again and again.

And again.

And again.

He had a big mouth that Robin was not going to put up with—especially not that night. As his mouth kept blabbing and words slipping, she threatened to push him off his bike if he didn't shut up.

A few minutes later, Robin slowed down her pedaling, and her bike got really close to Brük's bike. Brük's thinking, *All right, cool, she's flirting with me,* but she took her right arm, pushed him off his bike, and rode away. He promptly remounted his bike and rode the opposite direction, cussing her out as he went.

Thus began the love story of a lifetime, one that was without rhyme or reason, an attraction and bond that was unbreakable. Robin, the cute and petite blonde poet, was Brük's equal in every respect. Brük was tough and agile, a troubled guy who loved only three things: robbing places, drugs, and Robin.

Robin got home that night to find her ex there—a big Boston guy with a thick Boston accent saying things like *beeah* instead of beer or *gahbidge* instead of trash. He was trying to get back together with Robin, which was something she was not going to tolerate. But she did agree to allow him to stay at the house until he found a place under the one condition that he'd help her find this guy named Brük.

The two went down to Hyde Park and eventually found

Brük walking around. Robin paid her ex fifty bucks to "get lost." The Bostonian ex-boyfriend turned to Brük and said, "Just dahn't kiss her, man, 'cause that would be disrespectful. You know what I'm tahwkin' abahwt?" The two made their way back to Robin's to play some cards, but Brük wasn't even done dealing before Robin went in for a smackaroo. He said he couldn't—that he had just made a promise to that guy.

So began the first of many spats—always loud, semi-violent, and oddly endearing.

But it wouldn't take long for this new relationship to be put to the test. A few weeks later, Brük went to jail for driving on a suspended license, and when he got out, he went to Robin's house.

But she wasn't there.

Turns out both of them were looking for each other. She had recently lost her house and was now at the Salvation Army trying to get clean, but any chance she got, she would go to Montrose and look for Brük. She'd ask around and they would say, "Who doesn't know Brük? He just went that way no less than two minutes ago." And she kept missing him by only a few minutes and only a few blocks, like a train leaving the platform.

At the time, Brük was living in a garage apartment that, in order to get to it, you had to climb the tree of the house next door, jump over the fence and onto the balcony. It took weeks before Robin finally found Brük Dumpster diving in Montrose. For those of you who don't know, Montrose is a cultural hub, with mansions up against bungalows. It's been called the "Heart of Houston," the "strangest neighborhood east of the Pecos," and it was named one of the "ten great neighborhoods in America." What this all meant was you could find a lot of interesting not-so-crappy-crap in people's garbage. Brük once found a 1895 first-edition Ralph Waldo Emerson book of essays and was able to sell it for a good pocket of cash.

When the two reunited, it was incredibly short-lived. It wouldn't take long for the other one to find themselves checking into the "Greybar Hotel." You see, Brük would get a thrill from stealing bikes from the bike racks of high-rise condo buildings. Sure, for a while he'd do it for the money, selling these high-end bikes for enough to pay for whatever dope, weed, or booze he would need to get by that night. But after a while, he just started enjoying the high of the steal itself, so much so that he would sell the bikes for only five or ten bucks each.

But this one time he got his hands on a Sarasota bicycle, a top-end street bike. To ride this thing is like trying to drive a Ferrari at the speed limit. So, when he offered Robin a plain ol' mountain bike, she wasn't having it.

"Nah, man, I want that one."

But Brük wasn't giving it up. So, Robin popped him right in the mouth, and I think he might have even lost a tooth that night. I don't know if a neighbor called or the commotion itself drew the cops' attention, but, somehow, the coppers got over there, got Robin on the ground, and put the handcuffs on her. But what really got her in trouble was she wouldn't shut up (birds of a feather . . .) and so she got arrested for assault on an officer and was put in jail for the night.

Now the tides turned and the next day Brük headed back to his garage apartment to find a lock on his door and his stuff in a black garbage bag out front. Apparently, the guy whom he'd been staying with had been put into rehab by his family, and, without a lease, Brük was without a leg to stand on. He dragged his stuff to the curb, sat next to the Hefty bag, and snacked on some chips. When suddenly, who rounds the corner? Robin.

"What am I gonna do with all of my stuff?" he whined.

"Dude, we're homeless now. Fit what you can in the backpack and let's go!"

Their time on the streets was unique. They were social, clean, organized to the point of obsessive compulsion, and incredibly likable. Their escapades were more like Bonnie and Clyde than your stereotypical guy with a cardboard sign. In their first couple of weeks, they met Dennis Shaw, an eighty-something-year-old retired FBI agent who once worked on the JFK assassination. He was the son of a London-bred half-Indian father and an Englishwoman. This slightly chubby, suave, olive-skinned guy said that he had packed a ton of action in his time on earth thus far. He'd graduated from Rice and Harvard Law School, and his net worth was approximately seventy-five million, owning both a plane and a yacht.

Dennis apparently knew who Brük's dad was, an admiral in the navy, and the three of them would take his 1961 Lincoln Continental (the same make and model that Kennedy was shot in) to Riva's, a super high-end Italian place. Dennis would be wearing his tux or custom-made seersucker suit and bowtie, and would tell the two what kind of wine paired nicely with what entrée. After dinner he would ask, "So, what Dumpster shall I drop you two off at?"

The three of them would regularly go to the Hotel Galvez and drink at the bar until dawn, picking up other people's tabs along the way. One night, they had decided to drive to Galveston from Montrose—a fifty-four-mile trip that took them nearly eighteen minutes as they averaged 120 miles an hour down Highway 45—drinking orange juice and champagne in an Audi Q7. Robin was terrified in the backseat with her hands over her ears and eyes buried in her shirt.

The two would later find out that Dennis Shaw was actually Dinesh Shah and that he was a notorious con man known as "The Monster of River Oaks." Needless to say, he did not go to Harvard or Rice, he was not in the CIA or there for Kennedy's assassination, and he did not own a yacht or plane. As it also turned out, that was not his Lincoln Continental or his Audi Q7.

While living on the streets in Houston, Brük and Robin started going to a church service that provided food, and one day while giving his sermon, the pastor pointed at Brük and said, "You don't have to live like this."

Then he pointed to Robin and said, "You don't have to live like this."

The pastor went up to them at the end of the service and asked, "You two want to change? If so, we'll send you to this place in Kyle."

So the two went to Kyle. Robin was dropped off at the women's rehab and Bruk was dropped off at the men's. The places were miles away from each other and they were told that they couldn't communicate and they couldn't be near each other. Their first day, Brük couldn't find the backpack he came with that was full of clothes and a recovery Bible his father had given him. When he got word there was no halfway house to give them time to get on their feet afterward, Brük had a hunch they were getting scammed.

So Brük loaded up what he had left and walked out.

Minutes later, the women's house got a call and the staff told Robin, "Brük's left the house."

"Oh, then he'll be here any minute!"

"No, sweetie, he doesn't know where 'here' is."

Robin laughed. "I don't think you realize who this guy is. He's on his way here . . . *right now.*" She started packing and two hours later, sure enough Brük was walking down the road with his bags and twelve dollars in his pocket.

The two swung by a grocery store for a six-pack and a small, two-tiered grocery cart and started to make their way down the highway, pushing this cart with all their stuff and a pack of Old English. At this point they were three hours from Houston and only twenty minutes by car from Austin. So they decided to make Austin their new home. They got down to the next exit and began asking for rides at the truck stop. This one truck driver, a massive guy with tree trunks for arms and a sleeve of tattoos, said he didn't have room for them but gave them two moving blankets for warmth as he headed inside the station. A half hour later the same big guy walked out. He turned to Brük. "Look, guys, I just called my wife asking if it was all right that I took you guys and she said I couldn't, but I've been struggling with this since you guys asked me. So get in the truck and I'll take you guys to Austin. I'm an MMA fighter; I figure I'll be all right."

Twenty-two miles down the road, the lovebirds got off between a Wendy's and a Shell gas station. They started walking until they found a trapeze entryway, a little nook covered in a green-and-white checkered tile mosaic that was big enough to sleep in but didn't impede the flow of traffic.

A few days later on a late Friday afternoon, an old veteran

guy named Leo offered them some of his whiskey and said, "Welcome to Austin. Now you know you can't stay here, right?" Brük, ready to pick a fight, responded, "Who are you, old man?"

"Nah, kid, this is Sixth Street."

"What the hell do I care if it's Sixth Street? Seventh Street? Eighth Street?"

—◊—

A couple hours later the sidewalk was a flood of bar hoppers, bachelorette parties, and college kids. The two were forced to move along. After trying a number of other places that were not suitable or permissible to sleep, they ended up at a camp we established on the southeast side of Austin.

I had received an agreement for a little plot of land at the edge of a cliff with a perfect view of downtown Austin and right by the bus route so some of my homeless friends could have a safe and somewhat monitored place to sleep. It was an idea I had been mulling over for a long time—a community for the homeless to live and build relationships.

This was a pretty progressive camp—no one was allowed to be drunk or tweaking while on the premises or else they were kicked out for forty-eight hours (a rule put in place by the other campers). Brük and Robin's place in particular wasn't uncomfortable. When they moved out to the camp, Brük found a bunch of potting soil for sale, ninety cents a bag, and carried two hundred pounds of dirt into the woods to level the ground for their huge sixteen-by-fourteen-foot tent. They fully furnished the deal with an air mattress that converted into a couch, a coffee table, décor, two dressers, and a battery-powered vacuum. The tent was burgundy and cream, so Robin found a burgundy-and-cream rug, as well as a burgundy-and-cream plastic plant to tie the whole thing together. Needless to say, everything was perfectly organized and immaculately clean, and their motivation for normality and comfort was second to none. It was the tidiest camp I'd ever seen. Their personal hygiene was impeccable too. The two of them would not go a day without a shower. They used a square carton gallon of water, poked holes with a hot wire coat hanger at the bottom, filled the carton with hot water, and held it above their heads to get wet, then put it down, lathered up, and turned it upside down to rinse off. In the winter they would get dry as fast as humanly possible, oftentimes washing their bodies and hair separately to avoid pneumonia.

Brük was the only one motivated enough to make sure the camp always had a fire burning, one of which burned for eight months straight. He had two perfect stacks of wood—one for burning and the other for cooking. I called his signature scent *Eau de Char*.

We had set up a little area at the camp for dutch ovens and would even host lessons occasionally. But to truly impress upon you the extent that the two of them went to create a home, Brük found a two-basin sink down by the gully that he dragged out and cleaned up and then he framed in the sink between two cedar trees and used some PVC pipes to drain the water to the creek. He had taken some trashed two-by-fours and put in some shelves to store pots and pans, threw a tarp over it and a sheet of plastic behind it, and cut open a window—because Robin would not have a kitchen without a kitchen window.

Eventually, we hooked them up with a travel trailer, and a few months later, Robin was pregnant. It wasn't a week after their little girl was born that the two got in one of their spats: the cops were called, Brük was arrested, and CPS came to pick up their newborn daughter. Tricia got a call and headed down to the RV park to see what was going on. And she was not even really well-acquainted at the time with either Brük or Robin.

Robin didn't want her baby in foster care, so Tricia offered to let the baby stay with us.

Now, when Tricia came home with this seven-day-old baby named Avery, I knew we were stuck with it. I thought about the reality of Brük and Robin getting it together. I knew that recovery is a losing battle almost 100 percent of the time, and I was not prepared to have a newborn baby in my fifties.

So on day one with Avery, I was kind of pissed, and I started doing the math, *All right, I am fifty-five years old; I'm going to be doing Girl Scout camping trips at seventy years old! I'll be taking her to college at seventy-three! I'll walk her down the aisle at eighty!*

Day two, I looked at this little girl sleeping in-between Tricia and me, and I thought, *Okay, she's pretty cute.*

And by day three, I was hooked on Avery. There was a period when I felt disrupted that when I got home I had to deal with a newborn baby, considering I had already dealt with this four times over when I had my own children. I thought when they all left for college that my hands were clean and my child-rearing days were through. But it took less than one day before the love that permeated from this little peachy bundle of joy took over. It reminded me that no human life could ever be an inconvenience—not little Avery, whom I expected to raise to adulthood, and not troublemakers Brük and Robin. I love Avery. Tricia loves Avery. All four of my kids love Avery. And as it turned out, Brük and Robin loved her too.

—⁓—

After a couple days in jail, Brük and Robin came over to bring clothes, food, diapers, toys, and a crib, not allowing us to buy even the littlest thing. CPS allowed them to visit once a week for a supervised hour, so we told them that we were going to bring Avery to the commissary every day so they could see her when they wanted—which turned out to be all day, five days a week. They were elated that we had allowed them to see their daughter, and we were elated to see them as such loving and wonderful parents. They had both entered rehab, were working hard to prove their parenting abilities, and both were undergoing an obvious transformation. All the while the CPS and social workers were keeping an eye on them.

Five months later came their court date, and Robin had bought this flowy dress and little ruby red slippers for Avery. The CPS attorney stood up and said that Brük and Robin had done nothing but positive things. Avery's attorney said they were doing a great job. The social workers got up and said they made great parents. It was unanimous that the Keeners would make a happy little family.

Finally, Brük and Robin's attorney stood, holding Avery and describing how happy a baby she was. Avery then wiggled her little baby feet in the sparkly red slippers and the attorney said, "I know if Avery could talk she would say, 'There's no place like home.'"

The whole courtroom cheered, and the judge agreed with the attorney that there was no place like home for Avery.

Having those five months with Avery was such a blessing for me—to experience such warm and genuine love from her. In fact, this relationship with Avery is one of the most rewarding things that has ever happened in both my work and my personal life.

Currently, six years later, the three of them live in a beautiful three-bedroom home with a little terrier dog, Mr. Scruff. If you ask them what's kept them together for nine years, their first answer will be something about how "it is illegal in America to kill your spouse." But they'd follow up with the answer "patience, kindness, tolerance, and love."

Patience.

Kindness.

Tolerance.

Love.

These things culminated in a blonde-headed, blue-eyed Avery.

We know artists by their creations: Caravaggio by *The Incredulity of Thomas,* Led Zeppelin by "Stairway to Heaven," George Lucas by the Star Wars saga. Each masterpiece reveals something of its creator, and the same is true of God.

We catch a glimpse of the Artist at work by reading the very beginning of the Bible. He spoke galaxies into existence, formed the mountains, filled the oceans, and planted forests with a brilliant range of color and variety. You can see His playful side in creatures like seahorses, skunks, and flying squirrels. But the masterpiece that reveals more about God than anything else shows up when God made "family."

I know I keep saying it, but if you can ingrain one thing in your head, it's this:

> The single greatest cause of homelessness is a catastrophic loss of family.

Once we realize that this is the case, it reorients the thinking of how we are able to mitigate the problems we see in our society today. Make no bones about it—the issue is complicated. I imagine it to be like a multifaceted prism with multifaceted issues. Each issue is on the one side before it hits the prism, and we are interpreting that beam of light from the other side of the prism. So as the issues are being refracted, we each see the issue differently. There are many issues that most of us would agree upon. However, some of the issues are politically caustic. While people may disagree on abortion, we can all agree on the problems with foster care and the criminal justice system. There are issues around faith, single moms, single dads, divorce, poverty, adoption, and on and on and on. But unless we acknowledge the foundation, nothing we ever do will solve this pandemic. The foundation is the relationship that is first formed. The foundation is family.

Both Robin and Brük come from broken homes. Both had stepparents or foster parents. Most mothers would jump in front of a freight train to save their children; a few stepmothers would throw their stepchildren in front of a freight train. To be truthful, it's not necessarily the fault of the stepmother. It is an inherent human characteristic to protect our own. So when one of the parents leaves and gets replaced, the children are a little less "protected." The minute they start acting up, the level of frustration is one that might not have been there if both parents were biological—or if the children were "their own."

This is what sets Brük and Robin apart from the other stories I've told. Brük had a mother, a father, and a stepmother. Robin had a mother, a father, and a stepmother.

If I'm married and I have children, and then suddenly I make a decision to divorce my wife, go out and marry another human being, begin to sleep next to that human being, and then I have children with that other human being, you can't expect that other human being to have the same maternal bonding characteristics with the children whom I brought into the marriage that existed before her. In fact, the tolerance level for someone else's children is very thin. Whereas the tolerance you have for your own children is very thick. Both Brük and Robin were caught in that scenario as kids. It's a travesty in our society when that happens, because even though we convince ourselves that the kids are doing okay, they're not.

This isn't about making a judgment about whether or not their parents' divorce was right or wrong; it's about the collateral impact of those decisions on children. Brük and Robin were victims of that decision. So when their collective parents' behavior moved into a place where it became too caustic, the children were labeled as an inconvenience. It becomes easy for a stepparent to feel or say, "You aren't my problem."

If you have a family where the parents are both present and are the biological parents of the children, but the son grows up to have some issues, neither the mother nor father will want to abandon their son. Had the union broken up, it's possible the new wife or husband would say, "I'm not tolerating it. It's either me or him—but remember, you're sleeping with me."

Remember, I came from a divorced family. I get it. I still have bitterness in my heart about my father and stepmother and the decisions they made regarding how my brothers and I were to be raised. I'm sixty years old and still have grief for my father, my stepmother, and my mother who was essentially abandoned. And guess what? I was Brük and Robin. I was stealing cars, smoking pot, snorting coke, dropping acid. No surprise here. I had the father and the stepmother too.

I'll never forget one time I came home after school. I was seventeen years old, and my father brought me outside and demanded that I take the contact lenses out of my eyes so he could smoosh them on the ground. It was because I did not thank him for them. I looked at my dad as he spoke and heard the voice of my stepmother flowing through his teeth. I looked at his mouth and saw her mouth. So, I went to my room, packed up my stuff, and never went back. Today, now that I have my own family, I cannot even fathom how that could have ever unfolded, even if I was an ungrateful turd.

So about a year later, at eighteen years old, I bought a house that had a little house behind it, and I started reconnecting with my father and stepmother as my own mother was getting sicker and sicker. So I decided that she would live with me in the little house. This sent my stepmother into a tizzy. *I don't want her in this town. I've got roots in this town.* It was shameful, hearing this woman talk about my mother this way.

This catastrophic loss of family includes, at the subtlest level, divorce.

So, if the loss of family is the single greatest cause of homelessness, what *might* be the solution? When Brük and Robin realized that the three of them could have a family together with little Avery, everything changed.

Because family provides inherent roles that cannot be taken away. The minute you are born into the world, you become son, daughter, brother, sister, niece, nephew, and that, in some small way, provides an immediate sense of purpose. You become a good son or daughter, a good friend, and then a good mother or father. Our purpose, from the very beginning, is defined by relationship.

So if we can know Caravaggio, Led Zeppelin, and George Lucas through their creations, we can know Brük and Robin by Avery—an enthusiastic little girl who is too smart for her own good. Her life saved lives. Her very existence provided a little breath of fresh air. The combined spirit of Brük and Robin is what set up the two of them for success again. They felt purpose and unconditional love from their daughter.

But family is not only defined by having the exact same DNA. Tricia and I are committed to this family until the end. We love them. They're our kooky cousins, and, as their family, our goal is not to fix them. Our goal is to make sure that that the family avoids any more catastrophic loss of family—losing Avery or Avery losing them. We just come in every once in a while to provide support. When the solution doesn't come from a baby or marriage, it comes from us realizing our familial relationships—that we are all brothers and sisters needing to be reunited, needing to be there for our estranged family.

The addition of Avery resulted in a whole new branch of the family tree. Their family and the Graham clan joined together, and I was made godfather. This extension resulted in a natural restoration in which the house began to be repaired on its own—some cracks were filled, some upgrades were made here and there. We didn't mend the leaky roof, but we might have provided a ladder. We didn't fix all the broken windows, but maybe we at least removed the most broken one. Because how can you help a crumbling house if you don't get inside it?

Sure, it wasn't all peaches and cream once they got Avery back. They were in and out of jail, and we had Avery for a few more months later down the road while they were in rehab (again)—but the point is we have to be in the messiness. We want so badly to fix and repair broken people. Get them in, dust them off, smooth out the edges, and then have them go on their way. That's what their parents expect, and when that doesn't work, many parents leave. But the reality is we have to be in the mess and be willing to stay in the mess.

The mentality of drug addicts and alcoholics is entirely irrational until you understand that they are completely powerless over their addiction. Unless they have structured help, they have no hope.

Brük says he suffered from hopelessness more than homelessness. He had accepted that the tent and the woods were as lofty as he was ever going to get. Many people might respond to their behavior and mentality by saying it's a choice. *Stop buying the drugs! Stop getting into trouble!* And, in a way, they're right.

Perhaps addiction is not at the heart of disease.

Maybe homelessness is not the cause or result.

Hopelessness is. It's the sickness that often spurs the spiral.

Hopelessness is what causes you to lose the motivation to

PROV 29:18 NO VISION, REVELATION, GUIDANCE, OR HOPE
UNRESTRAINT, RUN WILD, PERISH

do any better. It's what causes you to lose any drive, ambition, or hope in yourself that you will do any better.

When Brük and Robin were still in their tent palace in the woods, Brük had bought a suitcase lock. And that resulted in a huge sense of pride—that they could zip up the canvas and then lock it like a door to create a line between the world and their own personal place. As time went on, the keys got a little bigger when they got the RV, and then another RV, and then they bought a truck—a hideous thing with a shark fin and hand-painted with the name "Shark Moble" (missing the "*i*" and forever being institutionalized in the Mobile Loaves Museum of our Minds as "The Shark Moblé"). Then the keys got a little bigger again when they got the manufactured home, and now, nine years later, they've got a remote for their garage door. They have a beautiful kitchen with four walls and a window above the sink. They have a living room where little Avery has her toys all put away in a chest. They have photo albums from their younger days of camo pants and Doc Martens. Avery even has her own little room with costumes. In an hour she'll change from Mrs. Claus to a cowgirl, to a Disney princess, to Dorothy playing with oranges that stand in as the Cowardly Lion, the Scarecrow, and the Tin Man. In that little room, to this day, she says, "There's no place like home."[1]

Robin has a box full of poems she has written. My personal favorite—which I feel sums their story up pretty nicely—goes like this:

> On my key chain hangs the key.
> The key of life, our destiny.
> The key a gift from you to me.

The key to my home, to be free, to me.
The key created my family—
Brük, Robin and ***Avery***.
Together we are ***Bravery***.
The key made possible a family tree,
A wish I thought would never be.
From the heavens appeared the key,
The key God used to set us free.

CHAPTER 9

WILL LANGLEY THE CARPENTER

HE STOOD IN THE DOORWAY OF THE OFFICE BUILDING AS HE took a drag and looked outside, shaking his head, "Nope."

Will Langley doesn't like to talk about his childhood—especially when there is a lady in the room.

We said we were going to meet at 1:30 p.m. to finally discuss what's been weighing so heavily on Will's shoulders, but at 1:27 p.m., as I turned the corner about three miles from where we said we were going, I saw him standing on the side of the road with a cardboard sign wearing a red and black flannel button-down over a *FILTER Magazine* T-shirt and blue jeans. His long white hair fell far past his shoulders and his beard was scruffy and unkempt. I eased on my brake, honked, and pulled over to pick him up, knowing he had forgotten. I looked in the rearview mirror, and watched as he jogged pitifully down the highway. He finally bent over, coughed, and walked the rest of the way to the truck. He's my age but has this awesome rock star hair and is somewhat of a cross between Jesus and a biker—both in appearance and personality.

Will used to be a beast—a guy with beautiful, thick, black hair and dark skin, an image of authority and masculinity. We used to call him "The Marlboro Man" back when he stood upright and his mustache was trimmed to perfection. Now he's gaunt, his left cheek missing from a removed abscess, and he coughs every five minutes from the asthma.

"C'mon man. We've been friends for nearly ten years and you still won't tell me the whole story."

"Not when Mama's in the room. It's too graphic." He nodded at my wife. "Besides it makes me too angry. I'm fine 'til I start thinkin' 'bout it, and then I start naming names. That'll just get me in more trouble. You know I like gettin' in trouble, Alan . . ." He winked and smiled a toothless grin, the kindness and wrinkles in his eyes making it the best smile I've ever seen, like a friendly jack-o-lantern.

"Yeah, I don't like it. I just don't like talking about it. God knows I can but . . ." His voice faded and he started staring off at some distant cloud or bird or something. Allergies had been bad at the time, and I couldn't tell if it was the cedar or the memories that made his eyes wet. He leaned his head back against the doorframe, the late afternoon sun outlining a silhouette and you can tell he was transporting back to his dark bedroom. He was returning to the small, shy, passive, notoriously gentle kid he once was.

It was July 1965 and the heat of a summer's day in Dallas, Texas, refused to relinquish its grip as night descended like a dark velvety sheet. Will didn't know what had just happened. He didn't understand what this man had wanted him to do. But he was exhausted and out of breath and in pain. The sweat had pooled in the middle of Will's back and his dark black hair lay tangled and matted across his damp forehead. His face was in his pillow, making it difficult to breathe.

The twin bed creaked as the overweight man stood fastening his belt.

Since the age of ten, Will Langley was pimped out by his father to other male pedophiles.

This happened on a regular basis for five years until Will was old enough and strong enough to fight back. How do you get over something like that? You don't. So, when the passivity slipped away like a fistful of sand, it was replaced by a rock of aggression and hostility.

When Will was fifteen, he started working at the gay bar his mother owned, making enough money in tips to fund his anti-depressants that cost less than a dollar a pop in 1970. Actually, they only cost about seventy-nine to nintety-nine cents depending on the brand (Piels and Pabst were cheaper than Budweiser). The anti-anxiety drugs cost a little more, seven bucks an ounce, but the Texas Tea would, at the very least, momentarily replace his anger with hunger.

But a few days into working at the bar, his passivity was proven to still be alive and kicking. His manager called him into his office and said, "Kid, you ever get really high?" He waved a needle in the air.

"No . . ."

"Well, stick out your arm, and turn your head away." Before Will had a chance to do either, the guy had grabbed his arm and jammed a needle in his thick, blue-green vein. Will looked down at the crease of his arm and his vein was swollen and red. That was the moment that sentenced Will to thirty-six years of living on and off the streets.

One funny thing about Will Langley is that he doesn't seem too bothered with it. He mainly just wants a roof over his head for the sake of peace and to wash his long Jesus-esque hair.

The other funny thing about Will Langley is a few years ago, we tried giving him an RV and a job as head of maintenance, but two months after move-in day he just up and disappeared for a year and a half. You think you can solve homelessness economically. You think you can give 'em a job and a house, but that most often doesn't work out too well. Sometimes, giving them a house is just putting a Band-Aid on a carotid artery. Some people need more flexibility in their life than the grind of an eight-hour job. Will is one of those people.

I met Will a few years after the organization's founding.

I had enough money to support my family for a couple of years, but money was tight, and our future was unknown. Our house started showing signs of wear and tear—roof leaks, side panels peeling, paint chipping—and so I met Will by referral. A friend from church who had been remodeling her house had used Will for all carpentry purposes and had high acclaims for this "homeless carpenter guy."

Turned out Will was an eleventh-generation carpenter.

Did you catch that? A few more and his ancestors might have shared a workshop with Jesus Himself.

His skills had come naturally to him when he was given his first hammer at the age of four. He was one of those folks on the streets that in the event of Armageddon you would want in your tribe. Actually, I think I'd want my tribe to exclusively be made up of homeless folks, because they are some of the most resourceful and resilient folks in the world. In the toughest of times, they know how to survive. Will is, unlike most people I know, a *naturally* gifted person. You give him an impossible project and he'll figure out a way to do it. He's the guy who will come into a homeless camp and immediately be elected as leader—he's tough, practical, resourceful, and honest. He'll figure out how to get rid of trash when there is obviously no trash service. He'll figure out the best way to keep your stuff dry during a downpour. Your tent's broken? He'll fix it.

Will builds homes for others while not having one for himself.

Doesn't that remind you of another carpenter who also, as Matthew 8:20 puts it, "Has no place to lay his head"?

Surely you saw this coming.

I'd say that my favorite pastime is wiping clean the cultural lenses that cloud our understanding of who Jesus is. Now, we all know that Jesus was a carpenter—the word being used was *tektōn*:

> Is not this the carpenter (*tektōn*), the son of Mary and brother
> of James and Joses and Judas and Simon? (Mark 6:3 ESV).

> Is not this the carpenter's (*tektōn*) son? Is not his mother
> called Mary? (Matthew 13:55 ESV)

Now, *tektōn* simply means "workman."[1] The Bible only states that Jesus was a laborer who performed physically demanding and socially shameful jobs. Jesus was a blue-collar worker, a peasant, and man of humble origins. If you take only one thing with you after reading this, please realize that Christ did not look like what we in today's society value. He is not—and never would be—the guy in the sharp suit working His way up the corporate ladder. He's just the carpenter guy with the old Levis and an unkempt beard, too busy trying to feed Himself and His neighbor than be worried about replacing His razor blades.

I know it's been said before.

I know it's a simple and clichéd use of imagery.

But for some reason people just can't accept it.

Think about the irony: Will Langley builds homes but doesn't have one of his own. And without a secure home, it's quite difficult to participate in society. This goes beyond getting a shower in before going to work, making a nice meal at the end of the day, and so on. They can't participate because they become so isolated in their own minds.

Think about it. There's an unsettling factor in not being home. We should understand that just because we have a house and four walls doesn't necessarily mean we have a home. Anyone can be unsettled. If you really want to understand homelessness, you first have to understand what it means to be home, and, incredibly, that definition doesn't include four walls and a roof. A typical post–WWII suburban home on a cul-de-sac with the front porch the size of a postage stamp and six-foot-tall fences for ultimate privacy does not a home make.

Well, there are only two things you need to understand

about homelessness in order to be more informed than the people running homeless shelters and nonprofits.

First off, in order to understand homelessness, you need to understand the eight essential characteristics of what it means to be home.

1. Home is a place of permanence (not just a roof above your head).
2. Home is a dwelling place (a place made of memories and relationships).
3. Home is a storied place (lots of laughter and tears).
4. Home is a resting place (a place you feel safe).
5. Home is a place of hospitality (where you can welcome others and others can welcome you).
6. Home is a place of inhabitation (where you nest and settle).
7. Home is a place of orientation (providing direction to our lives).
8. Home is a place of affiliation and belonging (a place to gain identity).[2]

Second, it's realizing that every human being is deserving of a *home*—that no one falls outside of the need for this basic right.

Once you understand this truly and wholly, you are better off than most of the CEOs running nonprofits! You can find your certificate at the end of the book (just kidding).

The problem is that, for some reason, most people cannot hammer or drill this into their head. They cannot understand what it means to have a home—that it is profoundly more complex than four walls. They cannot understand that everyone needs a home in order to function in the way we were designed to function.

We were designed to function relationally, not transactionally.

People may exclude the prostitute or the drug addict when the reality is that it is *especially* the prostitute and the drug addict who need a home (most likely because they might have never experienced it).

The "solution" is actually pretty easy.

In Roman Catholic teaching, there is a construct called *subsidiary,* and in Neo-Calvinist rhetoric, there is something called *sphere sovereignty.* So, good news: These are philosophies that Protestants and Catholics actually agree upon and share! In simple terms, it says that when we're dealing with profound human issues, we need to manage, deal, and attack them at the lowest social level. And the lowest social level and foundational "sphere" is the *family.* That is the foundation and original social cell of all societies. So, if the family has been obliterated by a nuclear bomb, like Will's family was, it's up to the "village"—the community—to help alleviate (you guessed it) that profound catastrophic loss of family. Now, what's happened at the village and community level is that we have abdicated these human responsibilities to city hall, the state government, and Washington, DC. And these entities, as important as they are in our society, are the least capable of dealing with profound human relationships. If you believe in mitigating homelessness and bringing palliative relief to

those suffering on the streets, then you believe in th
of relation, not transaction. You believe in friendship, nou
funds. You believe in love as ultimate shelter.

The government can only perform a transactional
model, so the only people that Washington, DC, can truly
help are the people living in Washington, DC.

Humans are difficult to repair. So, when families, even
intact families, abdicate the responsibility of their drug-
addicted family member, to whom do they abdicate this
responsibility to?

You are leaving a human life to chance.

What if nobody takes him in? What if I say, "He can't
live with us"? Everybody is looking for a fix, and the only
"fix" is to stay in the mess.

Now, this obviously won't cure homelessness, but it will
certainly alleviate it. It will definitely provide relief for a few
human lives. Rather than a division between justice and
compassion, we need compassionate justice. Remember the
definition of compassion as exuded in Laura? Compassion
means to *suffer with.* The call to justice is always a matter of
recognizing the pain and oppression in the life of another,
of sharing the pain in one's own life, and then of bearing the
image of the compassionate God by embracing the pain and
instituting ways of life that will alleviate that pain.

Do you see a thread here? It's called relationship. And if
we want to alleviate the pain associated with suffering, we
have to become intimate with that suffering individual.

There's this one little story about a bunch of nitpicky tools.

One day, the tools in a carpenter's shop were having a discussion about Hammer. When Hammer came over, the other tools informed him that he must leave, because he was too noisy. But Hammer said, "If I have to leave this carpenter's shop, then Gimlet has gotta go too. He's insignificant and makes a very small impression." (A *gimlet* is a tiny tool for making small holes). Gimlet stood up and said, "Ha! Okay, fine, but Screwdriver has got to go too. You have to turn him around and around to get anywhere with him!" Screwdriver turned to the other tools in the shop and said, "If that's what you really want, I'll go, but Plane has got to get out of here too. All of his work is on the surface; there's no depth to what he does." To this Plane leveled his pithy reply, "Well then, Saw will have to leave too. The changes he proposes always cut too deep." Saw complained, saying, "Ruler will have to leave if I leave, 'cause he's always measuring other folks as though he were the only one who's ever right." Ruler then surveyed the group and said, "Fine, but Sandpaper doesn't belong here either. He's rougher than he ought to be and is always rubbing people the wrong way."

In the midst of the argument, the carpenter walked in. He had to get some stuff done, so he sat down at his workbench and got to work. He used the ruler, the saw, the plane, the hammer, the gimlet, the screwdriver, the sandpaper, and every single tool in the workshop. When the day's work was over, he had made a beautiful wooden table. Though the complaints against each of these tools were absolutely true, the carpenter used every one of them.[3]

We are all purpose-filled individuals picking apart other purpose-filled individuals because their purpose and individuality looks different than ours. When we see a saw being compared to a hammer, we laugh at how obvious the comparison might be, and yet we don't see the silliness in comparing someone else's existence to ours. This is how the image of God in which we were formed has become marred and corrupted. The only conforming that needs to be done is conforming and reflecting God's innermost nature in our lives and accepting not only our purpose, but also the purpose of others.

Remember that there is no dichotomy between a human and God's image. Whoever abuses a human being, whoever ignores a human being, whoever hurts a human being abuses, ignores, and hurts God's image.

I have seen the absolute beauty of who Will is as a human being: his generosity, his work ethic, his willingness and desire to serve others, his desire to be part of a team, his desire to be admired. I have seen him in a place where he meticulously cares about who he is and what he appears to be—and any time drugs and alcohol are ever in the picture, we can tell merely by a single misplaced hair on his head. Every time that leads to the side of Will that society doesn't want to have around. But when we discard that part of who Will Langley is, we are simultaneously discarding the same parts that make him a great human being. We can't have it both ways. In Matthew 20:21–22, a bit of a revelation occurs among the disciples that there is something special about Jesus. There is something special about this kingdom. But being the "Doubting Thomases" we are, the full reality doesn't occur until post-resurrection. And so, a mother requests on behalf of her two sons, "Grant that one of these two sons of mine may sit at your right and the other at your left in your kingdom" (v. 21).

Jesus immediately and aggressively responds, "You don't know what you are asking. . . . Can you drink the cup I am going to drink?" (v. 22)

Truth be told, that mom was probably the smartest and best mom ever.

The two sons respond with, "We can" (v. 22). But I doubt they knew what they were getting themselves into.

Christ was asking in this moment, *Can you drink from this cup? Can you taste all the sorrows and joys? Can you live your life to the fullest?*

What I often ask myself (and what many of us ask) is, *Why? Why drink from that cup?* There is so much pain. So much anguish. So much violence. Why would we ever drink from that cup? It is a hell of a lot easier to live comfortable lives with maximum pleasure.

Henri Nouwen wrote a whole book about this moment in *Can You Drink the Cup?* In it, he explores the actual action and meaning of drinking from that cup and the weight it bears.

> Drinking the cup is more than gulping down whatever happens to be in there, just as breaking the bread is more than tearing a loaf apart. Drinking the cup of life involves *holding*, *lifting*, and *drinking*. It is the full celebration of being human.[4]

You can't drink from the happy or joyful side of the cup. When you drink it, you've got to drink all of it. When we are in a relationship with other human beings, we have to be willing to drink and take in everything from that cup. And if I'm going to be in relationship with Will, I have to take both. And just like Mr. Nouwen said, it is one full-on celebration of humanity.

I mean, thank God that Christ was 100-percent human—suffering and joy included. You can't have one without the other. Humans, roses, and nails have this in common.

To construct a human, to construct mankind, to construct the image of God and the existence of Christ, you have to have the rose *and* thorn; you have the sharp edge of the nail that pierces and the very thing that builds something new and repairs a broken thing. It holds it all together. Christ was everything—the culmination of thorns on His head and nails in His hands. His head full of roses and His hands prepared to rebuild.

In *Mere Christianity* C. S. Lewis used the parable of reconstructing a building to describe God's work in us—changing a house into a home:

> Imagine yourself as a living house. God comes in to rebuild that house. At first, perhaps, you can understand what He is doing. He is getting the drains right and stopping the leaks in the roof and so on; you knew that those jobs needed doing and so you are not surprised. But presently He starts knocking the house about in a way that hurts abominably and does not seem to make any sense.

What on earth is He up to? The explanation is that He is building quite a different house from the one you thought of—throwing out a new wing here, putting on an extra floor there, running up towers, making courtyards. You thought you were being made into a decent little cottage: but He is building a palace. He intends to come and live in it Himself.[5]

So if we maintain the idea that we are representative of different carpentry tools, God's rebuilding might look like using a lot of us to renovate—to drink from the cup that is full of joy and suffering. It takes a lot of roses and thorns and nails. For me, it is people like Will who turned my soul from a decent little cottage to a palace where God Himself dwells.

Therefore, if God dwells in us—if we are a living house—we better make sure God feels at home. That God is permanently there to dwell and allows us to feel as if we, too, belong in His kingdom.

The other notable thing about Lewis's parable is that not only does it talk about human restoration, but it also alludes to an earthly one. It looks to the final vision of homemaking where all men and women recognize that they are called to live in unity. With Lewis's words in mind, think about this: rough-and-tumble Will Langley's favorite things to make are hope chests—beautiful oak and mesquite hope chests for storing and collecting things in anticipation of the life to come.

In fact, when we encounter the Will Langleys of the

world, they build in us the ability to collect things in anticipation of what's to come.

With this idea of hope and rebuilding, I started looking for a whole bunch of acreage to help steward this ideal home.

CHAPTER 10

Taz Williams Ripped
His Blue Jeans

LARRY WILLIAMS FELT GOOD WALKING TO FOURTH GRADE wearing a brand-new pair of blue jeans—they were fresh, crisp, and still a dark indigo blue. Getting a new pair of jeans that wasn't a hand-me-down or worn after years and years of wear and tear was a big deal.

As he was walking across a field at recess, he saw this guy picking on this girl. So Larry rushed over, jumped on the kid, took him down, and, in the heroic process, skinned his knee on a rock. Yep, and right at the knee was his exposed bloody skin through a fairly small, though widely noticeable, rip in his brand-new blue jeans.

The minute he got home that evening, he was doing everything he could to hide this rip from his father—he walked into the kitchen with his backpack in front of his knee and sat at the far side of the table, crossing his other leg in front of the rip, while moving common household objects to obscure the tear. But he could only keep it up for so long. And it was in a moment when his motivation slipped that his father saw it, called him over, and asked how he ripped his new pair of jeans.

"This girl was getting picked on at school, so I beat up the guy who was picking on her."

As his father fell silent, Larry knew that no excuse was going to save him now. He closed his eyes tight and flinched, trying to anticipate where the blow would fall. Would it be a slap to the face? A kick in the legs or stomach? Would he be thrown to the ground? The silence was brutal. Larry just wanted to get it all over with.

"Well, that's good, son."

Larry's eyes opened, and he couldn't believe it.

The night continued calmly, and Larry climbed into bed still shocked at how well his father took it. While Larry was asleep, only a few doors down his father plugged in the flatiron and left it on for the entire night, and just like his father's temper, it was getting hotter and hotter and hotter.

So right when Larry woke up, his dad grabbed hold of his forearm and pushed the hot iron down into his pudgy arm. Larry screamed as his father pulled the iron away, the skin dripping off like melted wax, leaving the smell of burning flesh hanging in the air. This indescribable smell would haunt Larry for his entire life, accompanied with a triangular scar that took up his whole forearm.

Larry screamed, begging his father to leave. His father laughed and said, "No doubt I will."

If Larry were to summarize his childhood by a smell, it would be burning flesh, booze, and cigarettes. His dad was a cliché, a man who would go out for cigarettes and not come back for two years.

Other days, the Williams boys would be in a car. The car would break down, and the dad would go to get a new tire and just leave Larry and his five brothers on the side of the road with no intention of returning until weeks, months, or years later. The boys then had to make their way back home on their own. Once, Larry and his brother were left at a gas station, and the two of them lived inside of a water tower for two days until his mother realized what had happened.

Larry loved his mother. He and his brothers would always listen to her and do whatever she said. She was an immigrant from London and would try to get jobs here and there as a seamstress when their father was away in order to survive. They tried to take care of her, bringing home stuff they had stolen and rationing it out between the seven of them. They'd get a big bag of rice and a big bag of beans, and they'd eat off of that for as long as they could. However, his mother, being a religious woman, would force them to return anything she thought was stolen. So Larry and his brothers got smarter in their response: "Oh, we started working for Mr. Crabapple next door, and we're making some money from him."

So when Larry left home, theft equaled survival, and it eventually became a craft. He would hijack liquor and cigarette trucks as he jumped the rails and joined the circus. This is when Larry became Taz, short for, of course, Tasmanian Devil—a seething, snarling, insatiable lunatic. He was a muscle guy who no one wanted to mess with.

But the funny thing about this big, strong, stocky guy is, even at his worst, there was always this element of remorse for the kinds of stuff he was doing. One cold and windy night, Taz and his buddy came upon a church. His friend looked at Taz, opened his eyes real wide, and lifted his eyebrows up and down, and Taz said, "No, no, I'm not breaking in there." But his buddy started breaking down the door. Taz followed him in to get out of the cold and lay down in one of the pews, not paying attention to what his buddy was doing. He heard some rustling, and Taz lifted his head from the bench to see that this guy was holding the cash box and was running out the back door, yelling, "C'mon, Taz, someone's coming!" This memory haunted Taz just as much as the smell of burning flesh, in many ways likening them to the same thing—his humanity just melting away.

Despite his past of thievery and despite his hulking appearance, Taz was mostly known as being sweet, shockingly loving, and famous for giving the kind of bear hug that people don't get enough of. The kind that completely envelops you in warmth. The kind that reminds you that you really are loved. While on the streets, a bunch of Lay Missionaries of Charity, an organization that stems from Mother Teresa's movement, took him under their wing. This little group of ladies adored Taz, and through seeing their lives and work, he eventually converted to Catholicism—he confessed (which he warned would take a good two hours at least), got reconciliation, and took Communion.

From that moment on, he was never the same man; even while he lived on the streets, he lived a transformed life. He kept an index card underneath his pillow that said, "I love you, Jesus. I love you." I know he prayed it every day. He would do anything he could to make amends for his past, even so much as finding his father and telling him, after so much abandonment and so much abuse, "I love you. I just don't respect you."

This was the Taz I met, I knew, and I loved. This was the Taz who immediately became one of my closest amigos of all time.

Houston introduced him to me on that same day I met

Marge (the woman whom Houston embraced and whose hand I shook, not knowing that handshake would change my entire trajectory).

His ability to manage and ensure that the camp was always safe and secure was impeccable. It was from the seed of Taz that I realized that people we see from the outside as being totally dysfunctional—those who are disposed of and outcast—could live in community together. It made me start thinking that all of the lives I'd gotten to know could live in community. Not only could they live in community, they would thrive in it. And, furthermore, not just exist among each other, but people like me would want to know these teachers of reality, people who drink from the cup of joy and suffering better than anyone.

It seemed no coincidence that two of the most impactful people in my life, Taz and Houston Flake, lived together in community on the streets of Austin. That through Houston taking me by the hand and leading me to the other side, I would meet Taz. Taz's friendship eventually led to the idea to start cultivating some land to house over 250 people. I wanted to provide permanent, supportive, affordable, and sustainable housing to the chronically homeless based in a loving and hospitable environment, incorporating an understanding of what I'd seen in the RV parks that had an inherent quality of "community" that arises when people live in close contact with one another in dignified homes. I wanted to build a village of tiny homes and RVs, a church and a farm, and different ways for my friends to earn an income through woodworking or blacksmithing or making art. I would call upon architects to build beautiful microhomes—the goal being that people would want to live there. Who wouldn't love that?

So I started looking for one perfect piece of land that ended up being about the *fourth* tract that we looked at.

I think God likes to show off by equipping the unequipped. When you look back at the lives of the saints or holy people, or people whom we really admire, most of them come from backgrounds where they weren't equipped to do what they were being asked to do. I mean, Augustine was a sexaholic, but saints are sinners who keep on trying, right? (At least that's what I keep telling myself.) But my thread was being pulled to do something I didn't quite feel equipped to do.

One might call me the Village Idiot.

Our initial idea in 2006 was to get the city of Austin to collaborate with us. I knew that the city had tens of thousands of acres of land under their control. So, why not parcel out ten or twenty acres for a dollar a year so that we could develop a community that would have a profound impact on the city itself (and vice versa)? Seemed obvious enough. When I developed this idea of a KOA (Kampgrounds of America) on steroids, I pulled some city plans and asked an architect friend of mine to draw the design of the community and set up a model home at Midtown RV Park, where I brought Mayor Will Wynn to show him the plan and lay out the strategy on the table. I told him that we only had two requirements: (1) that it must have the entitlements to do what we wanted to do—water, electric, sewer, zoning, etc.; and (2) it must have reasonable access to public transportation. I told him, "If you do that, Mr. Mayor, we will raise all the money it would take to do this." First words out of his mouth were, "We need four of these around the city. One north. One south. One east. One west."

The second thing out of his mouth came as quite a shocker.

He told me that his grandfather was an alcoholic homeless man who was hit and killed by a car on the corner of Sixth Street and Red River. Me coming to him—asking him to build this community—was a healing moment for him. Since I had the go-ahead, I went and met with every other city council member. Mike Martinez (who at the time was relatively new on the city council) was the man who took it on. We found seventeen acres of land out east on a street called Harold Court.

In April 2008, the city voted unanimously to grant us a long-term ground lease on that piece of property. We were stoked. Blueprints were being drawn. The team was excited.

That's why I like to think that what happened three months later in the middle of summer was the heat and not the hearts.

We went to a neighborhood meeting, shared what we were doing, and it turned into war of the worlds. It was terrible. The police were called. It was aggressive. It was ugly. It was a circus. There was spitting. The media was there and people were yelling, but Mike Martinez got up and told everyone that he knew this wouldn't be a *popular* decision—and that they probably wouldn't vote for him when elections came around—but it was the right decision.

They answered with a typical *"not in my backyard"* response.

Now, the kingdom response would have been not only *"Yes! Absolutely in my backyard"*—which metaphorically means the surrounding areas—*"but inside my fence and as close to me as possible."*

The kingdom response is to welcome our brothers and sisters home. In fact, Christian hospitality transcends social and ethnic differences by sharing meals, homes, and worship with people of different backgrounds. The early church was known for including the poorest and the neediest—the people who could not return the favor. A better life is lived when you recognize the stranger in your midst. This implies not only respecting the humanity and dignity of the stranger, but also our common vulnerability and suffering. This is more than just providing the basic needs—food, clothing, and housing—but also recognizing strangers as our companions and friends. To invite the stranger to set aside his strangeness and become a friend.

It's this kind of hospitality that made Taz the single most loving guy I've ever known. If we were to give a scorecard to every person I know of how many of the eight essential characteristics of home they embody, Taz would have the highest at a 7.5 at least. It was incredible (though not surprising) to me that on one side you have the people in these neighborhoods who will not let a certain kind of person even live *near* them, and then you have Taz, who would always have a pitcher of fresh-squeezed lemonade for visitors. Taz was the guy who, when he finally did have an RV, would fill it to the brim with friends from the streets on cold nights, even if it got him in trouble. He would make a huge pot of hot chili and give everyone a bowl. You couldn't walk into his home without him making you a plate of food, pouring you a drink, and sitting beside you wanting to talk. Taz was the guy who would buy discounted Christmas cards in bulk in January and start handwriting letters in October so the 250 people on his list would get a heartbreakingly beautiful Christmas card, each personalized with what that person meant to him, along with a memory from the last year.

At eight o'clock the next morning, I got a call from the assistant city manager, saying, "Mike is calling a press conference at noon and would like you to be there. We have to postpone finalizing negotiations on this for a year." This put a bullet in the head of our plans.

It was depressing.

It was a giant setback.

Or was it?

The Mobile Loaves team was moving very fast at the time to get everything ready. And then—*bam*. We had the rug pulled out from under us.

As we were trying to recover from that setback, we started looking at the second piece of land by the Austin-Bergstrom International Airport, which turned out to be a part of the original airport acquisition and needed FAA releases.

Strike two.

So we checked out a tract near a particular high-end shopping mall. But before we got any further, that information was leaked to the press, which opened up a big Pandora's box. Once again I was going to neighborhood meetings and being cussed at, spit on, etc. This time even bigger players in the community attended, saying, *"We don't want this in our backyard."*

Strike three.

At that point in time, we realized it was going to be a struggle to get this done through the city. You can look at the right human thing to do, but there is also a political side. You can't dismiss the political side even though it might be contrary to the moral human side.

Time passed, and I went to the next mayor, Lee Leffingwell, and said, "Look, Mayor, I've got an idea, but I want to run it by you first. I'm going to go just outside the city limits of Austin—outside the main jurisdiction of Austin, where there is no zoning—and I'm going to buy a tract of land. This tract of land is going to have reasonable access to public transportation and utilities, but we're not going to have to deal with the not in my backyard mentality. But I want your permission to go and do that."

He looked at me and said, "You may very well be the smartest man I know."

So I went to the graduate architectural program at the University of Texas and gave them the parameters I was looking for as a class project. They went out and did a class search and came up with several tracts of land until we finally found the one. A crummy, crap-filled piece of land.

When I walked on that property the first time, the weeds went past my knees. A little dirt trail went through the property, and no matter which direction you went, you had to bushwhack your way through. About three tons of bottles, cans, newspapers, and car parts (over a thousand car tires, actually) covering the weeds. We made our way to the back of the property to find two stolen automobiles in the midst of being dismantled. The remains of illegal dumping were everywhere.

But, for some reason, God was calling us to that piece of land. It was just what we needed, and it had this calm aura surrounding it. Perhaps we needed to renew that land before we could begin to renew people, or even our city.

We immediately put the property under contract.

When you are under contract with zero dollars, it becomes a race trying to raise enough money. So, I was literally buying time, spending money I didn't have to keep that piece of property.

When the land was finally ours, we hauled away twenty

forty-yard Dumpsters of debris and more than one thousand discarded tires.

We walked all over it, we prayed over it, we circled it in prayer, we staked the corners with scriptures, we raised up a canopy in prayer, we put Protestant yin-yang, Catholic yin-yang, and Jewish yin-yang all over—whatever we could to make it a holy place. Taz, whose health had been deteriorating and was having difficulty walking, joined us as we walked around the weeds and the tall grasses and brush and asked if he could be the first resident to live in the village.

It was my honor to make him that promise.

The entire community began to come out to serve. More than five hundred volunteers, both with homes and without, would come out during the following weeks. Our dream of connecting human to human, heart to heart, was becoming a reality. This was not going to be a transactional housing model for the homeless. Instead, this was going to be a powerful relational model that would not only have a transforming impact on Austin, but also a gravitational pull for other cities with the same issues. So we called it the Community First! Village.

Taz was there from the beginning, his anticipation building right along with our planning. He watched as the grounds were cleared of garbage, the grasses mowed, the ground broken. He watched as the blueprints were drafted, as the architects and contractors inspected the land, with their pencils behind their ears—each and every tedious moment bringing him closer to home.

In the next few weeks, Taz started getting worse, so much so that they had to keep taking him to the hospital. You know how when you take someone to the hospital you never really expect them to die? This time I just had a feeling. I let everyone know. I sent out text messages and emails saying, "If you want to say goodbye to Taz, now is your time." What I didn't expect was for the hospital room to be filled to the brim with people from all walks of life. You had the coiffed and privileged, and you had the immobile homeless. You had the wife of the greatest living swim coach in the history of NCAA athletics next to drug addicts. You had the dentist who gave him dentures. You had multimillionaires, and you had missionaries.

There was a wide spectrum of people, as well as a wide spectrum of joy and sadness. All of us were laughing, crying, singing, and praying, some were walking in the room with guttural heaving, and nurses were having to tell us to be quiet. It is an image I will never forget for the rest of my life—that an alcoholic, drug-addicted, convicted felon can have that kind of impact on people. That room was just a sample of the multitudes of hearts he touched. When we bear the beams of love, we become more ourselves. We have to expect more for each other so that when we see the Juan Diegos and the Taz Williamses, we see impossibly red roses. Taz was an impossible red rose growing in the midst of the coldest winter. He grew out of the ashes. His life embodied the life of the repentant criminal, the crux of Christ's death epitomized, and the crux of my entire purpose for the Community First! Village.

Luke 23:39–43 says:

> One of the criminals who hung there hurled insults at him: "Aren't you the Messiah? Save yourself and us!" But the other criminal rebuked him. "Don't you fear God," he said, "since you are under the same sentence? We are punished justly, for

we are getting what our deeds deserve. But this man has done nothing wrong." Then he said, "Jesus, remember me when you come into your kingdom." Jesus answered him, "Truly I tell you, today you will be with me in paradise."

Think about it. The repentant criminal is technically the only confirmed person in heaven—the only confirmed saint. No one has heard out of the mouth of Christ, "I'll see you on the other side." This thief is the only person known to be in paradise after death—recognized by the Bible and, indeed, by Christ Himself. Based on everything we know about being blessed, everything we've learned about judgment, I love that this was where Christ first exercised this universal belief. That the criminal who was dying had just as much a chance, if not more, than any noted person in the Bible. Christ died for this exact kind of transformation, this kind of belief, and this kind of repentance.

In just a few moments, this former criminal went through sincere repentance. If we break it down, this guy did every transformative thing that the Bible asks of us when we become believers. His first concern was about his companion's wickedness in reviling Christ. "Don't you fear God . . . since you are under the same sentence?" (v. 40). Secondly, he fully acknowledged his own sin: "We are punished justly, for we are getting what our deeds deserve" (v. 41). Then he confessed Christ's innocence: "This man has done nothing wrong" (v. 41). He then placed all faith in Jesus Christ's power and will to save him. He turned and declared his belief in His kingdom. Then, he prayed. He cried to Jesus when He was hanging on the cross and asked Him right before death to intercede on his behalf.

Finally, in a rare and never-before-seen sense of humility, he begged to be "remembered" (v. 42).

Few people with all the time in the world have demonstrated such good evidence as this dying criminal.

So when Taz went to his true and final home, we planted a memorial garden in the village, and, to this day, it is the greatest thing out there. It started out as just a columbarium, but has become so much more and now represents the circle of life, a true and beautiful life that was no better exhibited than in Larry "Taz" Williams.

As you start walking through the garden, there is a playground that represents the beginning of life, which leads into a giant chess set representing the battlefield of life, the ups the downs, the victories, the defeats—but the fire pit, only a few feet away, represents the light of Christ. Then we have the prayer labyrinth that is constantly pulling us to the center, to the source of life. And at the center you have the columbarium right next to a large wooden cross. This isn't the cross of Christ. This is the cross of the repentant criminal.

All of this flows out of an alcoholic, a drug addict, a homeless man, and the first resident of the Community First! Village.

Remember the quote from Augustine, the sexaholic-turned-saint? "You stir man to take pleasure in praising you, because you have made us for yourself, and our heart is restless until it finds its rest in you."[1]

Well, Augustine brings this quote full circle near the end, saying:

At one time we were moved to do what is good, after our heart conceived through your Spirit. But at an earlier time we were moved to do wrong and to forsake you. But you God, one and good, have never ceased to do good. . . . [W]e hope to rest in your great sanctification. But you, the Good, in need of no other good, are ever at rest since you yourself are your own rest.[2]

Our circle of life is defined by utter restlessness without God and then ends with our rest in God. The Holy Spirit dwells within all of us and unites even the dying sinner. By sharing in God's life, believers will share in His rest for eternity. This is why the columbarium, where Taz lives and Peggy and Gordy live, sits next to the repentant criminal, the restlessness no more and union made.

When you zoom out of the memorial garden, now overflowing with the reddest forget-me-not roses and brightest flowers, you might look at and start thinking for a minute about how life is so short. You're born, you live, and you die. You enter the world, fight, and struggle, only to end up a pile of dust. Are we all just living to die?

When you look at all of our lives, we're often so aimless and our dreams so trite. It's when we find restfulness and home in Christ that we truly find life. When we are born out of the dust and given purpose.

Because aren't we all just dying to live?

Aren't we all just trying to find our way home?

CHAPTER 11

ELLIS JOHNSON'S JOURNEY HOME

IT WAS A SUNSHINY AUTUMN DAY AS CHUBBY SEVEN-YEAR-OLD Ellis Johnson sat on the kitchen counter, swinging his legs and mindlessly plugging and unplugging the electrical cord of the toaster into the wall. He was not thinking of much else other than plugging this bad boy in and then taking it out again. Like most seven-year-olds, Ellis didn't know the pyrotechnics of a toaster oven. After twentysomething occasions of him pulling out the plug, the whole thing sparked, caught fire, and began burning up the side of the wall. Ellis jumped down, got a bowl full of water, and threw it at the wall, saving the house from being engulfed by flames but leaving a black burn mark about three feet high.

`Ellis knew what this meant for him.

He ran up the stairs to his room, found the little nook between his bed and the wall, and waited as he fought off nervous tears and anxiously peeled the skin of his cuticles until he saw blood. For as long as Ellis could remember, he wanted to be a firefighter, so he felt proud of his fast instincts but felt stupid for causing the fire in the first place. Evening came and he heard his dad pull up the gravel drive. Ellis stopped his breathing, eyes wide shut, cowering.

He counted the steps his father made from the entry of the house and into the kitchen. *He's probably going straight to the fridge on the opposite end of the room,* he thought, *and he hasn't seen the burn yet. About now he's at the side of the fridge opening his beer with the bottle opener, and then right about now . . .*

"ELLIS, WHERE ARE YOU?" It wasn't even a question. It was a juddering demand. Ellis counted the stairs, hearing *one, two, three, four, five, six, seven, eight, nine, ten, eleven, twelve, thirteen, fourteen,* and then he heard his father round the corner and open the door.

"ELLIS." His father, recently retired, smelled as he always did—like beer. For a second Ellis thought back to before his father retired, when it was just he and his sweet mom at home all day—making lunch, reading books, going on walks calmly and quietly. Yes, Ellis had a great childhood until he turned five. His father, a cook in the military, was rarely home and resting was easy. But now he was retired, having nothing to do but drink and do what he was just about to do.

"Get your ass over here." Ellis's head rose beyond the edge of the bed and he made his way to his father, shaking.

"Did you make that mark in the kitchen?"

"Yessir."

Ellis watched as his father grabbed hold of his belt buckle, unhooked it from its fastening, and began to pull it through—loop, by loop, by loop—until his grip was on the middle of the belt. Now, sometimes his father would use the leather-strap end of the belt (painful stings that lasted through the night), and sometimes his father would use the buckle end (writhing bludgeons that would last for weeks). On this day he wore his silver military buckle—heavy with a carved eagle in the middle and an adorned frame that hurt all the more—and he went for the buckle side.

Ellis was facedown on the floor writhing, screaming, and begging his father to stop. His mother was in the other room, closing her eyes, wishing just as much as Ellis for his father to stop, and just as unsure what to do. She held her head in her hands and stood up to help, then sat down again in fear of what her husband might do if she were to intervene. Finally she heard a clatter, the buckle hitting the floor, and the father walking away, dragging the buckle through the hallway, the sound getting more distant, banging down the steps one by one—*fourteen, thirteen, twelve, eleven, ten, nine, eight, seven, six, five, four, three, two, one*—until she heard the sound of another bottle open and the recliner being put into a resting position.

Ellis was burning, his back torn to pieces, blood pooling here and there. His arms were outstretched, unable to pick himself up quite yet. He heard lighter footsteps make their way down the hallway and worried that his father was coming back for one more round, but finally he saw his mother in the doorway with a warm, wet washcloth to wipe his back. She helped little Ellis up and into bed, tucked him in, turned off the light, and shut the door.

The next morning, she woke him up for school and Ellis began to plead for her to let him stay home because his back still hurt. But she did not relent and off to school he went. It was a typical day in the second grade—math class, English class, then lunchtime (where he and his best friend talked about how Ellis wanted to be a fireman and his friend wanted to be a cop so they could save the world and help people), and finally gym class.

Of course, on that particular day the activities would include a riveting game of basketball—shirts versus skins. The teacher lined up everyone into a single-file line and began a pattern—shirts, skins, shirts, skins, shirts, skins—each kid assigned their team and parting in opposite directions. Ellis was desperately trying to count faster than the teacher so he could get out of line and switch before it got to him, when suddenly the finger pointed at Ellis and he heard a voice say, "Skins."

Ellis just stood there alone. His eyes wide and the cogs in his brain grinding and grinding, he desperately tried to figure a way out of the situation. The gym teacher said, "C'mon, Ellis. Skins." But Ellis, a child destined to beg, begged to be on the shirts team.

"No, Ellis. That's not fair. You got skins, you're skins. Take off your shirt and let's go."

So Ellis removed his shirt and let it slip out of his hand and onto the floor. As the game commenced he was not thinking about getting the ball, catching the ball, blocking the ball, or shooting the ball. He was making the most conscious effort to avoid letting any eyes fall on his scabby, wounded back.

But right when he thought he might get out unnoticed, the gym teacher called him over.

"Ellis, what happened to your back? Who did that to you?"

"My dad."

A few weeks later little Ellis Johnson, Mr. Johnson, and Mrs. Johnson were in a courtroom with little Ellis on the stand being questioned.

"Is there someone in this room who abuses you?"

Ellis looked out into the room and into his father's eyes, which were somehow silently demanding contact. Everyone else seemed to fade away and the two stared at each other, a battle for the ages. Ellis wanted his father to die, and he wanted to be the one who did the killing. So, little seven-year-old Ellis Johnson said, "No."

The lawyer's head jolted back, his brow raised, and the Johnson family went home, a devout trinity of dysfunction.

As Ellis ripened in age, so did his rage. He followed the footsteps of his dear ol' dad and left home at fifteen to drink, get high, and party. It was pretty harmless for the most part—some Lone Star, Mary Jane, girls, and a special "regular customer" certificate for his constant visits to the county jail—until one day he was in the basement of his friend's house doing what he did best: nothing. He saw his friend pull out a pipe and smoke something that smelled like nothing Ellis had ever tried.

"Hey, what you got there, man?"

"Man, this stuff will give you the best high there ever was. Try it."

If you were to talk to Ellis today, he would say that this moment is frozen in his brain. It was a moment that came cunningly, little by little, but as if it had always been there. He would say that this was the moment that changed the entire trajectory of the rest of his life. He should have taken a good look at everything one last time before that moment. There Ellis was, only twenty-two, still optimistic, social, wearing an oversized blue sweatshirt and a ball cap, his friend sitting on the grungy floral couch, and the smoke creating a natural vignette (like any dramatic memory would). Imagine a freeze frame with Ellis's hand extended, receiving the pipe that his friend passed.

Ellis brought the pipe to his mouth, inhaled, and let the smoke fill up his lungs as a strange feeling began to creep up his legs. His whole body was turning into an electric blanket and every little section of his mind was stimulated. Every fiber of his being was turned on. Like falling in love with himself. Everything inside of him suddenly seemed more and less significant.

It felt incredible to Ellis. But now he was stuck between a rock (literally) and a hard place in a soon-to-be never-ending grasp of the crack pipe's power. From that moment on he would chase the same feeling that he would never, ever be able to experience again.

The thing about crack is that it drains everything.

It takes your identity, your mind, your family, your friends. A few years later, before Ellis got a piece of him, his father died from cancer. While he was sick and weak, Ellis's father told him, "Well, look at me. Now's your chance, Ellis. I can't fight back." It was tempting, but Ellis couldn't do it. If he did he'd be no better than his old man. After his father died, Ellis moved back in with his mom. The two, while loving toward each other, were dysfunctional. They were all they had. The mother had her son, and the son had his mother. They were codependent. She would do anything for him even if that meant unintentionally fueling his addiction. He would do anything for him, too, so Ellis would go out and spend five to six hundred bucks a night on crack. When he'd run out of money, he'd go back to his mom, who would give him more money.

Until one day she didn't.

Like I said, Ellis would do anything for himself, and while he truly loved his mother, he feared that he wouldn't be able to chase the high. So the night she refused to give in, he took a swing at her. Thank God she dodged it, and his hand went through the wall. The pain in his hand jolted him back into the present moment—the reality of the situation—and he was able to see his dear mother sobbing and recoiling from her son.

He grabbed some things and left home, hitchhiking around Texas, getting high, and screwing off. It only took a few months until he was arrested. He had been in the courtroom a few times since that first visit when he was seven years old. There he was again on the stand. This time without a lawyer, his father dead, and his mother unaware that he'd been arrested again. The judge shook his head and said, "Ellis, I'm tired of seeing you in here and that's why I'm going to do you a favor. I'm going to put you in prison for two years and hope you come out clean and recovered. I wish you the best." The gavel banged and sealed the next two years for Ellis airtight.

The first year zoomed by. Ellis kept himself busy as the prison cook.

But the last year dragged along slowly, and Ellis counted the days until January rolled in. When December finally came, he was left with one month to go and he began counting the hours. Ellis felt ready for a new life—a clean life. *The judge was right!*

Then he got some news one week before Christmas Day.

Ellis's mother had died of cancer. Ellis didn't know his mother even had cancer, but then again, she didn't know he was in prison. Ellis, forced to beg again, appealed to the judge to let him go to his mother's funeral. But given the number of days left in prison, the judge told him he could wait to see his mother in the ground.

So the day he got out, that's exactly what he did. Seeing his mother there, buried right next to his father, wrecked him. He picked some flowers and laid them on the dirt-covered grave. His father's grave was overgrown, and he left it that way. He was unable to go back to the house, so he took his inheritance and moved to Austin, squandering the money on a series of crack binges for the sake of numbness. The fact that he was never able to apologize to his mother would haunt him for years.

Like the days he spent chasing crack, he also began running away from a life without his mother—days filled without meaning, wishing only to tell her he was sorry. He was sorry for the grief he caused her. He was sorry for asking for money. He was sorry for his short temper. He was sorry he ended up becoming his father. He was sorry for not being the son a mother hopes for.

And so the addiction relapsed.

He got some roommates and got a job as the fry cook at a drive-in down the street, a job he was able to keep until the manager's nephew pushed him over the edge. Ellis, now thirty-four, had been putting up with this kid's behavior—being elbowed in the back and side, teased because of his age, his frying oil occasionally and mysteriously missing during the busy hours. All of this Ellis was able to put up with. But when this kid said something about Ellis's dead mother, Ellis picked the skinny seventeen-year-old up by the shoulders and slammed him onto the grill, holding him there for a good five seconds before walking away. And yes, the grill was turned on.

Obviously, Ellis was fired. This was the catalyst for his eight years on the streets of Austin. But it also was the catalyst for the eight-year journey of becoming the man he was always meant to be. Most of us would assume that Ellis's life was over the minute he hit the streets; and yes, life as he knew it was. Nothing would ever be the same for Ellis. But this is where Ellis's story really began.

So began eight years of hunger. Eight years of sleeping near the labor center in hopes of getting some work. Eight years fighting hunger and fighting the hot summers and cold winters. Eight years of watching friends slip away from overdoses and suicide and hunger and the elements.

Ellis was desperate for community, tired of isolating others through drug use and depression. Ellis was desperate for dignified work to pay for a dignified life, tired of panhandling. Ellis was desperate for a meal, tired of reaching the brink of starvation and digging out of the trash to survive. A few months later, a friend told him that there was a truck serving food, blankets, and new socks in South Austin.

That's when he made the two-hour-long journey to the Mobile Loaves truck, and that's when I had the honor of meeting Ellis.

A six-foot-three-inch tall guy—quiet, shy, and fearful of eye contact. We sat down on a curb with a couple of PB&Js, and he shared his story as he picked at the skin of his thumb. It was immediately obvious to me that he wanted to work but lacked opportunities to earn an income. I had recently put the wheels on the idea of microenterprises out at the village. The hope was that this would provide dignified income opportunities and encourage our homeless friends to rediscover their God-given talents. Before long, Ellis was working as a vendor on a "Street Treats" mobile vending cart selling ice cream and snacks to hungry concertgoers. He also found work caring for the grounds at a local church and packaging socks with our friends at a sock company. Ellis ultimately found work that fed his soul as well as his belly in the gardens on our newly acquired land and eventually became one of the very first living residents at the community.

Most of the men and women in this book leave home because they believe they do not yet have a home, and therefore must look far and wide to find one. But home is the center of all of our being, where we can hear the voice that says, "You are my beloved. On you my favor rests."

It was a couple weeks before Christmas—a difficult time for Ellis, given the memory of his mother's death—the day he moved into his new RV. Thirty of us gathered around to throw a big welcome home party. Ellis started crying because this didn't just represent this moment of going from a sidewalk to a bed, from a curb to a couch, from a trash can to an icebox; it represented forty-nine years of homelessness—of not knowing his father, of loneliness, of aimlessness, of desperation. He cried because of all the people who celebrated this homecoming, thinking, *Wow, I must really be loved.* The welcome home party was a celebration of Ellis realizing who he is in light of God's love and human community.

What does *community* mean? Common unity. Realizing that we all are the same, no one is better than anyone else, and existing in that unified commonality. It's realizing that every single one of us can and should be able to identify with the feeling of homelessness—because we all have been homeless (and if you think otherwise, you are delusional, my friend).

Ellis's story is the ultimate, universal story of homecoming.

I'm sure you're all familiar with the story of the prodigal son. Daddy gives his inheritance to his sons, one son runs off, spends it on all the things he shouldn't, and when it's all gone he starts eating trash and sleeping with the pigs in the mud. When he's tired of doing that, he finally goes home to a father with open arms and a brother who is one big eye roll.

"There was a man who had two sons. The younger one said to his father, 'Father, give me my share of the estate.' So he divided his property between them.

"Not long after that, the younger son got together all he had, set off for a distant country and there squandered his wealth in wild living. After he had spent everything, there was a severe famine in that whole country, and he began to be in need. So he went and hired himself out to a citizen of that country, who sent him to his fields to feed pigs. He longed to fill his stomach with the pods that the pigs were eating, but no one gave him anything.

"When he came to his senses, he said, 'How many of my father's hired servants have food to spare, and here I am starving to death! I will set out and go back to my father and say to him: Father, I have sinned against heaven and against you. I am no longer worthy to be called your son; make me like one of your hired servants.' So he got up and went to his father.

"But while he was still a long way off, his father saw him and was filled with compassion for him; he ran to his son, threw his arms around him and kissed him.

"The son said to him, 'Father, I have sinned against heaven and against you. I am no longer worthy to be called your son.'

"But the father said to his servants, 'Quick! Bring the

best robe and put it on him. Put a ring on his finger and sandals on his feet. Bring the fattened calf and kill it. Let's have a feast and celebrate. For this son of mine was dead and is alive again; he was lost and is found.' So they began to celebrate.

"Meanwhile, the older son was in the field. When he came near the house, he heard music and dancing. So he called one of the servants and asked him what was going on. 'Your brother has come,' he replied, 'and your father has killed the fattened calf because he has him back safe and sound.'

"The older brother became angry and refused to go in. So his father went out and pleaded with him. But he answered his father, 'Look! All these years I've been slaving for you and never disobeyed your orders. Yet you never gave me even a young goat so I could celebrate with my friends. But when this son of yours who has squandered your property with prostitutes comes home, you kill the fattened calf for him!'

"'My son,' the father said, 'you are always with me, and everything I have is yours. But we had to celebrate and be glad, because this brother of yours was dead and is alive again; he was lost and is found.'" (Luke 15:11–32)

So which "brother" are you?

a. The "faithful," dutiful brother who stays home, works hard, and consequently has judgment and anger issues. He says: "Daddy! Watch me! Watch how hard I am working for you! Don't you think you should finally love me because of all I do for you?"

   b. The "loser" brother who could not care less about impressing anyone. He throws caution to the wind, but in the end he crashes and burns and returns home saying, "Father, I can do nothing to earn your love."

I hope for your sake it's Brother B, because the "loser" brother's sin is physical, obvious, and easy to turn from. In the end he doesn't even want to make those same choices. He is so overjoyed to be home. He is wholeheartedly repentant when he comes home. He realizes that he is deserving of nothing from his father. He is aware of his failures.

Like Ellis's addiction, he is aware of its inability to provide him a joyful life. Aren't we all addicted? Is that not the best word to explain the alienation epidemic that so deeply permeates society? We cling to what the world proclaims as the keys to self-fulfillment: accumulation of wealth and power, looking attractive so we can be affirmed of our value. These addictions create expectations that can do nothing but let us down, failing to satisfy our deepest needs. When we rely on these things, we live within the world's delusions, and our addictions condemn us to look for home in "a distant country," leaving us unfulfilled. In these days of increasing addictions, we have wandered far away from our Father's home.

Brother A, on the other hand, isn't aware that he is wicked, bitter, resentful, and angry. Brother A won't go to God and beg for healing from his condition because he sees nothing wrong with his condition. Man oh man, that's dangerous thinking. He thinks he's home just because he never left, but his heart is far from it. His true homecoming could only be found in welcoming Brother B home.

The truth is, you are Brother B every time you search for unconditional love where it cannot be found, in every earthly, material, human thing in the world. Think about your day and all the thoughts that pass through that brain of yours. Disapproval makes you upset. Praise raises your spirits. Rejection makes you depressed. The littlest success electrifies you. You are basically a tiny sailboat on the ocean, totally at the mercy of the waves. You're spiritually homeless. You've always had a home, in your father's house. The father wants not only his younger son back, but his elder son too. Yet you turned your back on him and chose to go live on the streets, in the rough-and-tumble world where people used you to get ahead, took advantage of you, and treated you however they wanted to. You've gotten used to living on those angry streets, wishing there was a better place to go.

There is.

Henri Nouwen's *The Return of the Prodigal Son* explores the parable depicted in Rembrandt's painting. He was so moved by the painting he began a deep meditation of what it was saying to him.

> The more I spoke of the *Prodigal Son*, the more I came to see it as, somehow, my personal painting, the painting that contained not only the heart of the story that God wants to tell me, but also the heart of the story that I want to tell to God and God's people. All of the Gospel is there. All of my life is there. All of the lives of my friends are there . . . How could I accept Jesus' call: "Make your home in me as I make mine in you." The invitation is clear and unambiguous. To make my home where God has made his, this is the great spiritual challenge.[1]

Turns out the word *prodigal* does not at all mean what we usually mean when we say it. It doesn't mean someone who returns after going away. It means someone who is completely spent with nothing left to give. And while that's the condition we're in when we realize our need for God, it also encapsulates God's love for us. Perhaps *prodigal* more aptly describes the *father* in the parable. The definition of the word *prodigal* is something like "reckless spendthrift" or "extravagant"—which are precisely the words that describe the love of God the Father. And this is Jesus' point when telling the parable.

Surprise! There's an option C.

c. The father. Someone who not only is forgiven, but forgives. The one welcomed home, but also who welcomes home. The one who receives compassion and offers it as well.

It is far easier to identify with the sons—both so relatable and profoundly human, and our identification with one of them happens almost immediately. We place ourselves on a scale of human brokenness (though I think the irony is that rarely do the older brothers see themselves as the older brother). Jesus says, "Be compassionate just as your Father is compassionate" (Luke 6:36 CEB). Coming home and residing in the Father's house requires that you make the Father's life your own and be transformed in His image—is this not the point of the gospel?

Becoming more human by becoming more like the Father?

When Brother B was no longer considered a human being by the people around him, he felt the profundity of his isolation, the deepest loneliness one can experience. He was truly lost, and it was this reality that brought him home—and in my experience, I can only imagine that the younger brother became like his father when he returned home. Because he understood. Because every son is faced with the decision to become his father. Because this is the story of every single story I've told thus far. Because after their experiences, they all eventually chose option C.

This is Houston's whimsy.

This is J. P. restoring that which is old.

This is David learning to wash feet.

This is Danny's constant generosity.

This is Peggy's uniqueness.

This is Tony's understanding of family.

This is Laura's compassion.

This is Brük and Robin's love for wholeness.

This is Will Langley's ingenuity.

This is Taz's culminated hope.

This is Ellis not knowing his father and not becoming his father, and this is Ellis knowing *the* Father and becoming the Father.

This is homecoming.

Ellis, being one of the earliest residents and the gardener at the village, is now the one who welcomes our volunteers and new residents into the village. He harvests the food and helps prepare it for our feasts. He is the one who came home and now says for all those coming home, "Let's have a feast and celebrate!"

The other day I found Ellis in the garden planting some olive seeds and simply asked him, "Ellis, how do you spend your days?"

"Well, Alan, I wake up. I read my Bible, have some breakfast and a cup of coffee, and I go out to the gardens and till the dirt to make sure all the plants have what they need. I teach some of the volunteers and residents how to plant, what different tools are for, and harvest some of the fruit and veggies that grow in the garden. Then I go back home and sometimes have some people over for dinner. It's Wednesday, so today we'll put all of what we've got in our fridge or what I have found in the garden into a pot and make a big stew and eat it outside. We'll all chat and share about what's been going on lately. Then I'll go to sleep in my bed and get a good night's sleep. I sleep easy now that I'm home."

I've always said that there isn't one thing in my life that I would take back or wish away. Sure, there are some things that I maybe *should* have done differently or things that I could have done better, but if given the opportunity I would keep everything just the way it happened. Because lives are made up of threads that seem disconnected, but when they cross over they are incredibly intertwined and tightly woven together. I hate that Ellis's childhood was rough. I hate that he experienced and has seen things that I can't even imagine. But I am perhaps selfishly grateful that those moments brought his thread over to mine so that we could have the friendship we have today.

Turns out that Ellis agrees.

He wouldn't change his childhood and wouldn't take back his eight years on the streets, because those moments brought him to the garden, to his family, to his home.

CHAPTER 12

END WITH THE BEGINNING IN MIND

The LORD God then took the man and settled him in the garden of Eden, to cultivate and care for it.

—GENESIS 2:15 NAB

IMAGINE YOU'RE STANDING ON PREHISTORIC LAND AND THE cacophony of cars, music, and voices have disappeared and been replaced with deafening silence. Pretend there is nothing to do but be on the earth—no distractions, no nine-to-five, no advertisements bidding for attention. You can hear every leg of every little bug touching every little leaf. You feel the direct, unfiltered sun so much that you can smell it. As you take a step, you feel the particles of earth being pressed against the other particles. Every sensory experience is tuned-in, and you are 100 percent present and aware.

Imagine that you are in the middle of nowhere, nestled

between two rivers. It's a quiet moment right before the sun rises over the hills, and you rise from your bed and have the ability to directly communicate with your Creator, thanking Him for this new day. You walk out to the garden and begin to till the earth, harvesting fruit and vegetables and planting new seeds for the next season. You feel no restlessness, no angst. Everyone and everything you love and could ever love is here.

We live here for a while, but like we as humans so often do, we screw up.

We can be certain, though, that being in the garden felt like home—a place of intended permanence, a dwelling place, a storied place, a safe resting place. The idea of home was perfectly and profoundly understood.

Since we were expelled, we've been desperately longing to return.

When humanity left the garden as home, what became of it? When we stopped tending to it and forgot its sacredness, what appearance did it take on? It's funny to think that the garden of Eden is likely sitting somewhere looking totally different. For all we know it could be a trash dump or a commercial hotel somewhere in the Middle East.

Though we don't know what has become of the garden of Eden, we do know what has become of us. Every single one of us has become wholly and irrevocably displaced. We were home, and we've been searching for and fighting for it ever since.

Now imagine that time lapses and days, months, and years zoom by. In the corner of your mind's eye, you see numerical years racing by chronologically—year by year. Imagine buildings rising and falling. People are zigzagging. There are little mud homes that wash away and morph into wooden houses that later rot and morph into brick dwellings that are torn down and replaced by massive skyscrapers. Children are born and grow into suited businessmen and businesswomen—people rushing in and out of coffee shops and banks and cars going in and out of massive parking garages at lightning speed.

Pause.

Here we are in beautiful Austin, Texas. It's a chilly night in January, and we are just south of downtown in Sunken Gardens—a park that has the entire skyline in perfect view and whose name perfectly suits its appearance and effect on your mood.

This is where I met twenty-five-year-old Jericho with a cigarette dangling out of his mouth. He breathed in and coughed; a rattling helicopter with a broken blade. He was excited about the new pair of sneakers he'd just received from the Mobile Loaves truck, as the pair he was wearing had given him blisters all along his ankles and he had recently acquired shin splints.

He had a fresh cut on his nose—too recently given to be a scar—with a bubble of fresh dried blood. Turns out someone with a high school class ring had punched him in the face and stolen everything he had—his laptop, his phone, and worst of all, his beloved guitar. His guitar meant everything to him. He said to me, moments after meeting him, that if someone offered him one hundred thousand dollars to never play a song ever again, he wouldn't take the deal. Not sure if that's the smartest decision or not, but I can respect it. My best bet is that he hadn't been on the streets as long as he let on because everything he had was lost due to trusting people to not take his things. He was a polite kid, only dropping the f-bomb when he

was really excited about something. He potentially had undi-
agnosed schizophrenia, an obsessive compulsion for picking
up litter and throwing it in the trash, and an Irish accent that
was obviously not authentic since he had grown up a few hundred miles away in Central Texas to American parents. He did
not know his biological dad, but he was sure that he was born
in New York.

He ended up acting as our enthusiastic tour guide while
on a recent Street Retreat—spotting good sleeping spots and
waving to his other homeless compadres, all while maintain-
ing a sense that he was the luckiest man alive to have gained
such a large number of new friends. There were about twenty
of us walking the streets, the majority of which were college
students. Since Austin is a city that's unfriendly to pedestrians,
it always exudes a sense of unfamiliarity and wonder to first-
time Street Retreaters. With spectacular alleyways opening up
like portals to unknown dimensions, the belly of downtown
swallowed them whole. For many of the kids in the group, this
was the first time seeing and meeting drug addicts and prostitutes while we walked like a serpent of trailblazers, a cartel of
story collectors.

On our trek we met Crystal, a woman who looked sixty-
three but was only thirty-six, had four children, and, an
abusive "boyfriend." But she still maintained a sense of faith
that was unparalleled. She slept underneath the University of
Texas Co-op on "The Drag" with some carpet she found, but
no blankets. She had broken her back a few months ago at a job
moving sacks of flour, but received some workers' compensa-
tion that helped pay for the surgery. She was in a lot of pain and
trusted no one.

We met Andrew who was sitting in the middle of Sixth Street soaking wet because the passersby were dumping their beer on him for a laugh. He was an autistic man, without friends or family, and unable to get a job. So there he sat until we came and befriended him and helped him move.

We met Ashley, the daughter of an abusive father and the sexual plaything of her stepfather—who had been raping her for years until she moved out when she was fifteen. She then got involved with drugs and started calling the sidewalk her bed. She liked ska music and macaroni and sweet tea.

As we turned corners and sat on curbs and lay in the grasses of public parks and caravanned through the city, we met the weary, the hardworking, the hungry, the abused, the neglected, the molested, the traveling, the tired, the hopeful, and the hopeless. We traded cellophane-wrapped baloney sandwiches from the pantry for unbelievable stories of anguish. We traded cigarettes for friendship. We traded Bundt cakes for handshakes.

—m—

Eventually all of the Street Retreaters, along with Jericho, made it back to the village. The interesting thing about Jericho (besides his quirks) was his name. It wasn't his actual name and he wasn't a seemingly religious guy. But this young postmodern nomad had—for some reason still unknown to me—decided to go by the name Jericho.

In the book of Joshua, the story goes that the city of Jericho was where the first battle of the Israelites was fought in their pursuit of the promised land. The other interesting thing about

Jericho (the place) is this is where the Israelites were rescued and sheltered by Rahab, a Canaanite prostitute. So the importance of Jericho is twofold: (1) the location of the first fight for the restoration of the promised land (an idea similar to what man was displaced from in the garden of Eden), and (2) the place Rahab—a woman many of us would be disgusted by, would judge, and would chastise—saved the Israelites (and it now serves as a symbolic foreshadowing of the *ideal* believer). She was not a likely candidate for a heroine of faith, but it's just like Jesus says, "The tax collectors and the prostitutes are entering the kingdom of God ahead of you" (Matthew 21:31).

The Battle of Jericho, in a way, was the first of many battles for our home. This is why the entirety of the Bible could be defined and summarized by *homemaking*. The theme of homemaking epically bookends the entire biblical story and human narrative. The Bible begins with Adam and Eve having a home, the middle is all of humanity looking for a home, and the whole deal ends with the beginning in mind—the culmination of home through Christ's return.

Everything about the Community First! Village incorporates a holistic approach toward this vision of ultimate homemaking—in particular, reuniting with our estranged family. It's allowing the tax collectors and prostitutes to enter first, because the Ellises and the Will Langleys and the Rahabs have a strong desire—just like the Jews did in Egypt—to be home. This is, in a way, their exodus out of the streets—out of an environment where they are unsettled, living under the girders of overpasses, and into a promised land.

We decide to hop on the Capital Metro bus and get off at the stop that's a mile away from the village in order to walk down the country road. It's a billboard-less road with only a single road sign that reads Hog Eye Road. On the north side is a tottering barn in a wasted field with half-weathered fences. Among the other visible fields, you can see a large tree—almost leafless now with its bare branches netting darkly against the sky. Then on down, where the road curves away, there is a village. *The* village.

We arrive at the open gates at the bottom of the hill and I ask young Jericho, "All right, bro, you ready to see something big?"

I begin a tour I've done hundreds, if not thousands, of times. A piece of land now speckled with different colorful tiny homes. Each little house is unique and designed by some of the most respected and renowned architects in the country. There are some quaint and homey yellow ones with big screened-in porches and rocking chairs. There are modern and minimalist wood and metal structures, Spanish casitas with stone walkways, and some with rooftop decks that are equal in size to the living space, begging to be filled with family and friends. Each house is fully furnished, not with Salvation Army throwaways, but with beautifully crafted furniture especially made for those who will live there.

The population is a mix of the formerly homeless and people who have left their homes in order to live a more minimal and quality life of community—some of these people are doctors or own multimillion-dollar companies and have chosen to sell their house and live in an RV or tiny home. And they're much happier for it too. Less, when it comes to anything but people and love, really is more.

There is a bed-and-breakfast filled with towering painted tepees, shiny airstreams, and vibrant campers. Born from the mind of a celebrated and legendary hotelier, it is designed so that visitors can come for the weekend, bond with our residents, help in the gardens, feed the goats, or learn a craft from one of the residents. It is all only feet away from the fire pit and state-of-the-art outdoor amphitheater that was donated by Alamo Drafthouse. (Thanks, Tim.)

We make our way past the Community Market and the Topfer Health Resource Center that provides not only regular mental and health screenings, but also hospice and respite care so that no one dies alone. We move toward the workshop that has a tool bank and art house. This building is dedicated to the microenterprise opportunities that give people the ability to hone their natural and artistic capabilities to make a dignified income.

There is a main hospitality center where visitors and residents can cook in the kitchen and all sit down at the wooden tables under the warmth of the glowing stringed white lights and eat meals together to share communion and *Communion*.

We walk a few steps forward to the farm where you see the happiest little coop in America providing fresh eggs and free-range chicken. There are goats that provide milk to make fresh goat cheese, beehives that produce fresh honey, and a catfish farm that uses an aquaponic system that naturally utilizes organic plants for nutrition. In short, this is the highest-quality local and organic food in the world—so locally sourced that it is steps outside of their front door and feet away from their kitchen.

In the heart of the village is the Larry "Taz" Williams

Memorial Garden, which includes the playground, a giant chess set, and a prayer labyrinth among beautiful flowers and plants.

There is a carpentry and blacksmith shop for classes and more enterprise opportunities. There is a tiny modern chapel tucked among the tiny homes, with a red door and copper sides and a stark white front with a stained glass image of the repentant criminal. There is a dog park with dog pools and obstacle courses nestled in the trees.

All around the village are hammock groves, bench swings, picnic tables, fire pits, and places for friends to gather. The entire village is encircled by a walking trail.

There is everything you could ever possibly need or want.

This is a twenty-seven acre, fourteen-and-a-half-million-dollar mansion with two hundred and fifty rooms. And guess what? We bought the twenty-four acres next door too.

When you zoom out, you see all the faces of the men and women in this book. These people are the heartbeat of the village. An aerial shot provides a tapestry of *life*. Of *my* life. This is everything I'd been working for. All along it was slowly being sewn together. Because every person I interacted with is a part of the person I am becoming. Houston Flake was my tour guide—the man who took my hand and guided me through the nitty-gritty in order to see what was truly beautiful and true about the world. You see J. P. in the fruit trees and nut trees—something that is available to every living person. You see Danny in the hospitality center and the picnic tables that are sprinkled around, encouraging each and every resident to share a meal. You see Peggy in the Art House—a place for people to express themselves and make a dignified income. You see Gordy in the giant playground, Laura in the tepees, and Will in the carpentry workshop. You see Taz in the columbarium and you see Ellis settling, cultivating, and caring for the garden and farm animals. You see a synchronized heartbeat of every life—every thread—intersecting. You see younger prodigal sons and happy older brothers. You see people coming home and people welcoming them.

Our dream of connecting human to human and heart to heart has become a reality. This was never going to be a transactional housing model for the homeless. People are not just objects to satisfy—*Here's your green soup; now go sleep on a cot.* We are meant to hold the promise of life to others. Start treating people with dignity and respect. Start doing that, and the world cannot—will not—stay the same, because people respond to being loved.

When I give tours of the tiny houses to people that *have* homes, I bring a little metaphorical bell. When they step inside they see a space with beautiful floors and handmade local furniture, light streaming in through the windows, structurally designed for natural cooling with airflow to minimize power use. Each has a covered porch so they can have guests over to sit and talk and be together.

Sometime during all of our tours of the village, someone who *has* a home, probably one that is ten to twenty times bigger in size, says, "I want to live here." That's when I ring that imaginary bell.

And I swear, I've rung it every time.

This is a place where everyone wants to be. It feels familiar. It feels like the home we've felt but never been to. It's *Sehnsucht* fulfilled. It's *inquietum* settled. This is a place of intended permanence, a dwelling place, a storied place, a safe resting place. The Community First! Village is a place modeled after the place we were displaced from.

Many often ask, "But what is it going to be like when you get two hundred and fifty of 'those people' on this property?" This question originates from deep in the stereotype library, from people assuming this place is just going to be like the gunfight at the OK Corral. My answer usually both simultaneously enlightens and stuns them. I respond, "It will be a lot like your family!" Their eyes usually get as big as saucers, knowing that most of our families are pretty messy. I add, "Yeppers, it will be messy." Funny, though, how this seems to resonate in a positive way. Life is messy. Family is messy. Community is messy.

Why should we expect anything different?

And when I step outside of the tiny house, I take my tour-goers to the edge of the property and tell them the single greatest problem in Western civilization is what is just beyond that fence—and I point at the suburb. Identical-looking homes with front porches the size of the newest iPhone and privacy fences that tower the height of your average human being. There's a community pool at the center of the neighborhood, but it's always empty because each house has its own private pool. If these folks do spend any time outside, it is in their secluded, protected, and isolated backyards.

That isn't home.

And I swear to you, they all get it. Every single person on that tour understands the problems and the weight with living in this space.

Thus, this groundbreaking community is a humble attempt of mirroring that ultimate home—what the Israelites fought for, what Christ will bring, and what we all anticipate. This picture of the new heaven and the new earth is a picture that has reality at the heart of it, but is beyond our imagination.

Pictures do that. They are more perfect than our imagination.

However, there are a few things that we can know for sure about the coming kingdom: we will be closer to Jesus, we will be the most full humans, we will be surrounded by a transformed creation, and we will live in that transformed creation with transformed bodies. Because the reality is that reality is *real*. It's material. It's physical and without bodies and material matter you cannot have relationships, and without relationships you cannot have meaning.

Which is also why the idea of physically beautiful and individual houses is important. Because the reality of what it means to be home is that these stories and memories and experiences in a home are often bounded by four walls. Stories and memories are set off by boundaries as the special places they are—as a *home*, with four walls and a covered porch and rocking chairs and the people who are invited in and share the space. Because boundaries are not where something stops, but where something begins at its essential unfolding.

At least that's what I tell myself about that six-foot-tall privacy fence. That it is the demarcation of homelessness and homefulness, and it's shocking when that realization sets in.

That is why the gospel is at the heart of this little plot of land in East Austin.

Paul says in 1 Corinthians 15:58, "Therefore, my dear brothers and sisters, stand firm. Let nothing move you. Always give yourselves fully to the work of the Lord, because you know that your labor in the Lord is not in vain." He is looking toward the new earth. He is talking about the work of love.

Because whatever the gospel is about, it is about *life*. Life that never runs out. Today, here, now, in anticipation of the new earth. Our work is rooted in relationships and intimacy with others.

Nothing about life implies the need to have a bunch of stuff. None of it goes with you when you die. I can promise you one thing for sure: The best things in life are the things that are alive. Ask anyone's favorite moments—it's being with people and being on this very-alive earth. The bugs crawling and grass growing. It's not the day they got their first phone or computer (and if it is, man, that's just sad). The things that matter are the things that need breath. Everything about your life should be about keeping the beginning of time in mind.

> Then the LORD God formed a man from the dust of the ground and breathed into his nostrils the breath of life, and the man became a living being. (Genesis 2:7)

> The LORD God took the man and put him into the garden of Eden to cultivate it and keep it. (Genesis 2:15 NASB)

It's about life.

Consider your life a rare and beautiful miracle and you'll start seeing everything as rare and beautiful. In the beginning was homemaking. In the end is homecoming. But homecoming can only happen if there was a home in the first place.

There is a popular book by author Stephen Covey called *The*

Seven Habits of Highly Effective People. Habit number two just so happens to be "begin with the end in mind." Makes sense. You want to start with a goal. You want to have the ability to envision what it is you want first so you can achieve it in the end.

And, sure, I agree with this. But I believe life isn't always about efficiency.

I believe in meaningful inefficiency.

I believe in the Jesus Positioning System that often takes you out of your scheduled, time-lined, beeping, dinging, and ringing calendar and into something much deeper and richer. Take time to stop and smell the bouquet of Christ.

So I believe in ending with the beginning in mind. I believe in keeping life and homemaking and homecoming and intimacy at the forefront of my thinking, and I believe in the power of doing everything I can to bring that home here. For everyone.

And you should, too, 'cause it's super awesome.

—∞—

Do people meet you and immediately think *I am home?* Is this how you come across to the people around you? In your work? In places where people rub shoulders and bump against you? If they don't, you have a problem, and if they do, then you are God's glory. By others feeling life from you, you in turn are more fully alive—more fully human.

So here's my final answer to the question of what it means to be a human being.

It's like Saint Irenaeus said, "The glory of God is man fully alive."[1]

Imagine that true goodness is not about rules, but a matter of living life well—of living a life of God. The goal is that people feel more alive after meeting us than they did before. That is what we are called to be—citizens of a new earth, living in anticipation of a glorious capital-K kingdom.

We learn who we are by looking into other people's faces. Mother Teresa said, "Only in heaven will we see how much we owe to the poor for helping us to love God better because of them."[2]

Ingrain these faces and human stories in yourself so deeply that you become who you are meant to be—so that you finally become like the image from which you were made.

Your life should be the story about your journey of becoming fully human. Your life should be about God breathing His breath into you to make life. It should be about God taking the form of man and walking out what it would look like as a living example. It is the ultimate protagonist entering the only real narrative in hopes to enter every one of our stories—every one of our threads—so that our streets can be filled with people who are fully being what they are called to be.

No longer strangers and aliens. No longer wandering nomads, purposeless tourists—no longer exiles and dispossessed, homeless vagrants.

All of this—Juan Diego's story, my story, the stories in these pages, the story of every living soul on this planet—is all to say that there is a reason the biblical narrative starts with a garden and ends with a city.

God can make all things new.

The city and the garden represent physical reconstruction, spiritual restoration, and divine recreation. Biblically (and from personal experience), what makes them both incredible—what makes a city spectacular and a garden beautiful—is when it is settled. When people fill it and make it and build it with the best that they can. When humanity builds beautiful buildings, restaurants filled with the most imaginative uses of ingredients to make gospel con carne, museums filled with beautiful works of art that share the stories of the human soul, and gardens—gardens that when settled and tilled result in red, red roses, fresh and flavorful vegetables, happy goats and rabbits and donkeys and chickens. This is a model for how we were always meant to live—a life filled with dignity, creativity, beauty, intimacy, and the joy of becoming fully human. This is a visual for how we can change our communities one human at a time.

It's about being on earth as it is in heaven.

Everything about how we interact with this world is about homemaking, and the entire point of Christianity is about *homecoming*.

And thus ends my tour. A rant-filled, always invigorating thing for me. Jericho soaked it all in. He fed the goats, pet the donkeys, and climbed the steps to explore all the tiny homes and not-so-tiny facilities. He jumped on rocks and swung on swings. He laughed.

That evening we have a bonfire over by the tepees and share some Lone Star beer, chips, and Hatch green chili salsa. Jericho is sitting in a wooden lounge chair, feet kicked up on the stone of the fire pit, his arms crossed behind his head, eyes closed, and smiling. Everyone around him is chatting and laughing, and he is just soaking it all in. His shaggy brown hair and impish face looks like how I imagined Ellis looked when he was young and wandering for nearly forty years. A younger, restless brother and an older brother with open arms. I can see trajectories—a life in and out of prison, wandering the streets for food and friendship, a life of desperation. Then, I could see a life of homefulness and happiness, of full bellies and rested heads and community. There he is, new to life on the streets, but still optimistic with dreams of becoming a rock star—a representation of the young generation of chronically homeless.

I go and sit next to him. "Hey, bro, what are you thinking about?"

Jericho pauses as he smiles and opens one eye. "I'm just so glad I didn't have to die to see heaven."

Welcome home.

Acknowledgments

TO MY FOUNDING BROTHERS—BRUCE AGNESS, PAT PATTERSON, Jack Selman, Mark White, and Houston Flake—thank you for your courage. God knew what He was doing when He brought the six of us together.

Decker, Taylor, Marlee, Keaton, and Samantha. You are the best ever.

Thank you, Brian and Betsy McClure, for your unbelievable generosity.

David and Kay Shiflet, you two embody the meaning of compassion.

Katie Zunker and the whole Mobile Loaves & Fishes staff—past and present. None of this could exist without you.

Matt Baugher and the entire Thomas Nelson team. Thank you for your belief in this message.

And most of all, thank you to all the men and women who taught me the true meaning of home.

NOTES

INTRODUCTION
1. See Exodus 3:14 and Matthew 25:40.

CHAPTER 1: THE THREAD, THE HEAD, AND THE HEART OF ALAN GRAHAM
1. G. K., Chesterton, *Irish Impressions* (London: W. Collins Sons & Co., Ltd., 1920), 203.

CHAPTER 2: HOUSTON FLAKE'S 400 POPSICLES
1. *First Things*, Dec. 1991, No. 18, 63.
2. "The Suicide of the Liberal Church," Chris Hedges, Common Dreams, January 25, 2016, http://www.commondreams.org /views/2016/01/25/suicide-liberal-church.
3. http://www.heri.ucla.edu/cirpoverview.php.
4. *Encyclopedia Britannica Online*, s.v. "cerebrum," accessed May 17, 2016, https://www.britannica.com/science/cerebrum.

CHAPTER 4: DANNY HENDERSON'S STREET NAME IS PREACHER
1. "Addiction: The View from Rat Park," Bruce K. Alexander, BruceKAlexander.com, 2010, http://www.brucekalexander

.com/articles-speeches/rat-park/148-addiction-the-view-from
-rat-park.

2. *Catholic Encyclopedia*, s.v. "corporal and spiritual works of
mercy," Catholic Online, accessed May 17, 2016, http://www
.catholic.org/encyclopedia/view.php?id=7903.

3. Mother Teresa, "One Strong Resolution: I Will Love," (speech,
fortieth anniversary of the United Nations, United Nations
General Assembly Hall, New York, October 26, 1985), verbatim
transcript by the Permanent Observer Mission of the Holy See
to the United Nations, New York, January 14, 2004.

4. Ibid.

5. Andrew Louth, "The Didache," *Early Christian Writings: The
Apostolic Fathers* (Harmondsworth, Middlesex, England:
Penguin Books, 1987), 192–93.

CHAPTER 5: PEGGY AND DAVID: THE BABY BOOMERS

1. Widukind Lenz, "The History of Thalidomide," (lecture,
UNITH Congress, Toronto, 1992), partial transcript at
"Thalidomide," Thalidomide Victims Association of Canada,
accessed May 17, 2016, http://www.thalidomide.ca/history-of
-thalidomide/.

2. Robert Karen, *Becoming Attached: Unfolding the Mystery of the
Infant-Mother Bond and Its Impact on Later Life* (New York:
Warner Books, 1994).

3. Ibid.

4. James R. Edwards, *The Gospel According to Mark* (Grand
Rapids, Wm. B. Eerdmans, 2002), 468.

5. Tacitus, *The Annals*, 14.42–45.

CHAPTER 6: GORDY THE GENTLE GIANT

1. "Meaning, Origin, and History of the Name Gordon," Mike
Campbell, Behind the Name, May 17, 2016, http://www
.behindthename.com/name/Gordon.

2. C. S. Lewis, *Mere Christianity* (New York: HarperCollins, 2000), 91–92.

Chapter 7: Laura Tanier Was an Engineer

1. F. Tobin, trans., *Mechthild of Magdeburg: The Flowing Light of the Godhead* (New York: Paulist Press, 1998), 153.
2. Henry Chadwick, trans., "Book I.i." *Confessions*, by Augustine (Oxford: Oxford UP, 1991), 3.
3. Walter Hooper, ed., *They Stand Together: The Letters of C. S. Lewis to Arthur Greeves (1914–1963)* (New York: Macmillan, 1979), 316.
4. Ibid.
5. C. S. Lewis, afterword, *The Pilgrim's Regress*, 3rd ed. (Grand Rapids: Wm. B. Eerdmans, 2014), 204.
6. *Merriam-Webster*, s.v. "compassion," accessed October 4, 2016, https://merriam-webster.com/dictionary/compassion.

Chapter 8: The Love Story of Brük and Robin

1. L. Frank Baum and W. W. Denslow, *The Wonderful Wizard of Oz* (New York: Penguin Classics, 2012).

Chapter 9: Will Langley the Carpenter

1. *The King James Version New Testament Greek Lexicon*, s.v. "tekton," Bible Study Tools, accessed May 17, 2016, http://www.biblestudytools.com/lexicons/greek/kjv/tekton.html.
2. Brian J. Walsh and Steven Bouma-Prediger, *Beyond Homelessness: Christian Faith in a Culture of Displacement* (Grand Rapids: Wm. B. Eerdmans, 2008).
3. "Inside Story: The Carpenter's Tools: An Allegory," *Sabbath School Net*, June 22, 2014, http://ssnet.org/blog/inside-story-carpenters-tools-allegory/.
4. Henri J. M. Nouwen, *Can You Drink the Cup?* (Notre Dame, IN: Ave Maria Press, 2006), e-book, 24.
5. Lewis, *Mere Christianity*, 205.

Chapter 10: Taz Williams Ripped His Blue Jeans

1. Chadwick, "Book I.i," 3.
2. Chadwick, "Book XIIII.xxxviii," 304–305.

Chapter 11: Ellis Johnson's Journey Home

1. Henri J. M. Nouwen, *The Return of the Prodigal Son: A Story of Homecoming* (New York: Doubleday, 1992), 15.

Chapter 12: End with the Beginning in Mind

1. John Eldridge, *Waking the Dead* (Nashville: Thomas Nelson, 2016), 10.
2. Shawn Madigan, *Mystics, Visionaries, and Prophets: A Historical Anthology of Women's Spiritual Writings* (Minneapolis: Fortress Press, 1998), 425.

About the Authors

ALAN GRAHAM IS THE PRESIDENT, CEO, AND FOUNDER OF Mobile Loaves & Fishes. MLF is a social outreach ministry committed to providing permanent, sustainable solutions for the chronically homeless with compassion, love, and dignity. Since 1996, Alan and teams of volunteers have been delivering meals with a side of hope to the homeless and working poor on the streets of Austin and have empowered other cities across the world to do the same. Since 2005, Mobile Loaves & Fishes has also been providing housing to the homeless through its Community First! Village. Founded in 1998 by Graham and five friends, MLF has served more than five million meals. With more than eighteen thousand volunteers, MLF is the largest feeding program to the homeless and working poor in Austin.

LAUREN HALL HAS WORKED AND WRITTEN FOR A NUMBER OF publications about art, film, and literature. She graduated from The King's College in New York City with a degree in media, culture, and the arts. She now lives in Austin, Texas, where, besides reading and writing, she likes to travel and wear many hats (both literally and figuratively).